Acclaim for

WOLFGANG SCHIVELBUSCH's

Tastes of Paradise

"Schivelbusch's stimulating history of the social meaning of various substances ingested or inhaled for pleasurable effect is itself a very pleasurable blend of historical detail, social analysis and unusual discernment. [A] gracefully succinct and very readable book."
—*Philadelphia Inquirer*

"*Tastes of Paradise* is a well-argued, briskly written and profusely illustrated account of the urge by the upper and middle classes of Europe to use stimulants not only for their own pleasure but also as measures of status. Schivelbusch shows that the seemingly little things do mean a lot."
—*Miami Herald*

"An imaginative cultural historian, Schivelbusch fits seemingly commonplace popular trends within the wider frame of economic and political history. It's an art at which he excels. This book is spicy, stimulating, and intoxicating."
—*Houston Phoenix*

"Tantalizing...Schivelbusch does not sit still in any one place for long. In this slim volume he covers a lot of ground. His narrative is spiced with enough quotations to lend authority but does not in documentation. Profusely illustrated, *Tastes of Paradise* is both entertaining and informative. Enjoy it."
—*Raleigh News Observer*

Tastes of Paradise

Also by Wolfgang Schivelbusch

The Railway Journey:
The Industrialization of Time and Space
in the Nineteenth Century

Disenchanted Night:
The Industrialization of Light
in the Nineteenth Century

TASTES of PARADISE

·

A Social History of Spices, Stimulants, and Intoxicants

·

WOLFGANG SCHIVELBUSCH

Translated from the German by David Jacobson

VINTAGE BOOKS
A DIVISION OF RANDOM HOUSE, INC.
NEW YORK

FIRST VINTAGE BOOKS EDITION, JULY 1993

English translation copyright © 1992 by David Jacobson

All rights reserved under International and Pan-American Copyright Conventions.
Published in the United States by Vintage Books,
a division of Random House, Inc., New York, and simultaneously in Canada
by Random House of Canada Limited, Toronto. Originally published in hardcover
in Germany as *Das Paradies, der Geschmack und die Vernunft*
by Carl Hanser Verlag Munchen Wien in 1980. Copyright © 1980 by Carl Hanser
Verlag Munchen Wien. This translation first published by Pantheon Books,
a division of Random House, Inc., New York, in 1992.

Library of Congress Cataloging-in-Publication Data
Schivelbusch, Wolfgang, 1941–
[Paradies, de Geschmack und die Vernunft. English]
Tastes of paradise: a social history of spices, stimulants, and
intoxicants / Wolfgang Schivelbusch; translated from the German by
David Jacobson.—1st Vintage Books ed.
p.   cm.
Translation of: Paradies, der Geschmack und die Vernunft.
Includes bibliographical references.
ISBN 0-679-74438-X
1. Drinking customs.   2. Drug abuse.   3. Spices.   4. Manners and
customs.   I. Title.
[GT2880.S3613   1993]
394.1'2—dc20   92-50603
CIP

Manufactured in the United States of America
10 9 8 7 6

To Christina Spellman,
stimulating breakfast companion

Sometimes, when I had drunk a lot of coffee,
and the least little thing would startle me,
I noticed quite clearly that I jumped before
I had heard any noise.

—Lichtenberg

CONTENTS

PREFACE

$\mathcal{T}$his book deals not only with the history of *Genussmittel* * —
the spices, stimulants, and other substances ingested or inhaled
by humans to produce a pleasurable effect—but more impor-
tantly with the question: In what way did these substances affect
the history of man? How is it that at certain times new luxury
food items appeared in Europe? Were coffee, tea, and tobacco
merely the casual results of colonial discovery? Or did they sat-

---

* The German word *Genussmittel*, literally "articles of pleasure," denotes a
group of substances for human consumption which are eaten, drunk, or inhaled
to create pleasures of the senses, as opposed to those foods and beverages consumed as necessities. They include all spices and condiments as well as stimulants, intoxicants, and narcotics such as tobacco, coffee, tea, alcohol, and opium.
The word *Genussmittel* therefore also implies that these substances are luxuries
for sybaritic enjoyment, means for creating epicurean delights and, by extension, a state of sensual bliss. —Trans.

isfy a need for new *Genussmittel* not previously available, and how can these new needs be described?

These are the general questions I shall take up here and from which other more specific questions suggest themselves for investigation as well. They are:

Why did the Middle Ages have such a pronounced taste for dishes seasoned with oriental spices, and why did this craving disappear so suddenly in the seventeenth century?

Why did the eighteenth-century aristocracy prefer chocolate as a beverage, whereas the bourgeoisie were fixated on coffee? How is it that in the eighteenth century tobacco was primarily snuffed, whereas before that it had been smoked in a pipe and, subsequently, in cigars and cigarettes?

Why, for centuries, were certain substances—for instance, opium and hashish—used freely as everyday items of pleasure, but then toward the end of the nineteenth century suddenly labeled as addictive drugs and prohibited?

The German word *Genussmittel* is somewhat misleading. The English and French languages come closer to historic reality with the word "stimulants." For these items did not serve merely for purely paradisiacal enjoyment. They always performed a "practical" function at the same time. Their historical function was this "performance-in-the-process-of-enjoyment" which at first sounds like a paradox. The effects they produced on the human organism were the final consummation by chemical means, one might say, of a course that had been well charted before in spiritual, cultural, and political ways. The morning cup of coffee and the Saturday-night tipple tie the individual into his society more effectively because they give him pleasure.

Tastes of Paradise

ONE

⁘

Spices,
or the Dawn
of the
Modern Age

⁘

$\mathscr{N}$othing could be more common than the salt and pepper on our tables. In our cuisine these two seasonings are always paired. Their containers are as alike as two eggs, indistinguishable except for the inscription on each. Yet in coupling them this way, two distinct epochs of world history are being conjoined. Salt and pepper represent two fundamentally different phases of human civilization.

Let's start with salt. Undoubtedly its first use dates back to dim prehistory. It is a primordial, sacred substance. The Latin words for "well-being," *salus,* and for "health," *salubritas,* both derive from the Latin *sal,* meaning "salt." The Romans offered salt to their gods, administered it as medication, and used it to preserve and flavor food. Elsewhere it enters the names of cities in areas where salt was obtained: Salzburg, Salzgitter, Salzwedel. In ancient Greece guests were presented with salt and bread as symbols of life and the sanctity of hospitality; and even today we give salt and bread to newlyweds when they set up housekeeping. The biblical expressions "the salt of life" and "salt of the earth" are still used in everyday speech; the more we take those meanings for granted, the less we know of their original sense. For us, salt is one of the cheapest commodities, the most plebeian of condiments; it may well seem strange to us then that the youngest daughter in the fairy tale should compare her love for her father to her love for salt: "Just as the best food is tasteless without salt, so do I love my father as much as I love salt."

Whereas salt has been a part of human civilization since time immemorial, the history of pepper can be dated more precisely. Actually the Romans already seasoned their food with it, but with the Christian Middle Ages a new chapter of universal significance began in its history.

The medieval ruling classes had a peculiar penchant for strongly seasoned dishes. The higher the rank of a household, the greater its use of spices. A cookbook from the fifteenth century gives the following directions for the preparation of meat: rabbit is prepared with ground almonds, saffron, ginger, cypress root, cinnamon, sugar, cloves, and nutmeg; chicken giblets are prepared with pepper, cinnamon, cloves, and nutmeg. Fruit is prepared similarly. Strawberries and cherries are soaked in wine and then boiled; next pepper, cinnamon, and vinegar are added. One recipe reads: "Cook a large piece of pork, not too lean and very tender. Chop it as fine as you wish, add cloves and mace and continue chopping, also chopping in dried currants. Then shape into little round balls, approximately two inches across, and set aside in a bowl; next prepare a good almond milk, mix in some rice and boil well, taking care that it stays very liquid. . . . Sprinkle generously with sugar and mace, and serve."

Although the medieval recipes don't specify any quantities, we can deduce from other sources how much was used. For a banquet with forty guests a late-medieval household account book lists:

"one pound of colombine powder . . . half a pound of ground cinnamon . . . two pounds of sugar . . . one ounce of saffron . . . a quarter pound of cloves and grains of guinea pepper (grains of paradise) . . . an eighth of a pound of pepper . . . an eighth of a pound of galingale . . . an eighth of a pound of nutmeg . . . an eighth of a pound of bay leaves." For festive occasions these quantities were substantially increased. When in 1194 the king of Scotland paid a visit to his fellow monarch Richard I of England, he received, among other tokens of hospitality, daily allotments of two pounds of pepper and four pounds of cinnamon, obviously more than one person could consume. Spices had a ceremonial as well as a culinary function here; in the Middle Ages the two were closely connected. Besides being used in food, spices were presented as gifts, like jewels, and collected like precious objects. Today we would attribute such dishes to an Arabic-Indian cuisine rather than to any western one. Prepared foods were virtually buried under spices; food was little more than a vehicle for condiments which were used in combinations we nowadays would consider quite bizarre. At especially refined tables spices became emancipated altogether from the prepared food. They were passed around on a gold or silver tray—the spice platter—during the meal or just after it. This platter was divided into various compartments, each of which held a specific spice. Guests helped themselves, adding spices as desired to the already seasoned dish, or they used the tray as a cheese or dessert platter. They consumed pepper, cinnamon, and nutmeg as we nowadays might partake of a delicacy, a glass of sherry, or a cup of coffee. And spices were not only eaten; they were also drunk in beverages. Medieval wines were more solutions or leachates of spices than the juice of fine grapes. They were boiled, like tea, with various ingredients and then decanted.

Historians have tried to explain this powerful medieval appetite for spices by pointing to the prevalence of inadequate food-preserving techniques. Pepper together with salt, it was said, was the chief means of preservation, of keeping the meat of cattle, slaughtered in the fall, edible throughout the winter. The other spices, according to this explanation, served to make spoiled meat edible again. This is hardly convincing, for spices imported from the Orient were among the most precious substances known in the Middle Ages. That is why they were the prerogative of the upper classes. To limit their function to food preservation and explain their use solely in those terms would be like calling champagne a good thirst quencher. Salt served very well as a meat preservative in the Middle Ages; and there were suitable native herbs which were also used by the poorer people to make spoiled meat palatable. So there must have been a different explanation for the appetite for spices of refined people in the Middle Ages.

The one thing that pepper, cinnamon, cloves, nutmeg, ginger, saffron, and a whole series of other spices had in common was their non-European origin. They all came from the Far East. India and the Moluccas were the chief regions for spices. But that's only a prosaic description of their geographic origin. For the people of the Middle Ages, spices were emissaries from a fabled world. Pepper, they imagined, grew, rather like a bamboo forest, on a plain near Paradise. Ginger and cinnamon were hauled in by Egyptian fishermen casting nets into the floodwaters of the Nile, which in turn had carried them straight from Paradise. The aroma of spices was believed to be a breath wafted from Paradise over the human world. "No medieval writer could envision Paradise without the smell or taste of spices. Whether the poetically described gardens served saints or lovers, the atmosphere was inevitably infused with the rare, intoxicating fragrance of cinnamon, nutmeg, ginger, and cloves. On the basis of such fantasies, it was possible for lovers and friends to exchange certain spices as pledges of their relationship" (Henisch).

Spices as a link to Paradise, and the vision of Paradise as a real place somewhere in the East—their source—fascinated the medieval imagination. The exorbitant price of spices, which reflected the extremely long trade route from India to Europe, further enhanced this fascination. Pepper, cinnamon, and nutmeg were status symbols for the ruling class, emblems of power which were displayed and then consumed. The moderation or excess with which they were served attested to the host's social rank. The more sharply pepper seared the guests' palates, the more respect they felt for their host. This symbolic value appears also in the use of spices beyond meals and banquets. They were presented as gifts of state, and were bequeathed together with other heirlooms; in fact, pepper frequently took the place of gold as a means of payment.

The symbolic meaning and actual physical taste of medieval spices were closely intertwined. Social connections, balance of power, wealth, prestige, and all manner of fantasies were "tasted": what would become matters of social and cultural "taste" or fashion, were first matters of physical tasting. Meanwhile, the ability of people in the Middle Ages to discern social and cultural circumstances through the tasting of food came to be a completely natural, almost unconscious ability. We need only consider the connotations that sweet and dry wines conjure up today, backed by an entire social hierarchy of tastes. In the early Middle Ages, before spices had begun to take on their role, European taste had not yet been sensitized in this way; it was still dull—numb, so to speak. Spices were to give it that first and historically decisive refinement.

The role which oriental spices played in the cultural history of medieval taste is part of a more comprehensive pattern of development—a matter of taste in the broadest sense of the word: taste which the West would begin to cultivate in the high Middle Ages.

In eleventh-century Europe a new way of life was beginning to emerge, a new and unprecedented interest in beautiful objects and elegant manners. Up to that time the feudal society of the West had been more or less a backwoods agrarian civilization. The castles were little more than large fortified farmsteads, just as the life and conduct of a knight were as yet scarcely different from those of a peasant. Lords and vassals wore clothes of similar materials and ate similar foods; in short, the social and therefore cultural separation between them was relatively small. These primitive conditions changed but slowly, in the course of centuries. More and more, feudal lords developed a lifestyle intended to increase the distance between them and their subjects. Everything coarse and plebeian became anathema. The refinement of etiquette and of the objects of everyday life became one of the most effective means of separating the classes.

But let me point out one special aspect of all this refinement: it was *not* essentially an indigenous product, but an import, obtained from the same source that supplied those spices which were themselves a significant, indeed perhaps the most significant, element in this cultural change. Like the spices, all the other trappings of this new upper-class culture came from the Orient.

In the high Middle Ages "Orient" meant Arabic civilization, which Europeans first encountered extensively through the Crusades. Trade with the Orient had existed before; in fact, it had never totally ceased since Graeco-Roman times, though in the early Middle Ages it dropped to a bare minimum. But only through the Crusades did the Orient become a reality for Europe. The Crusades began as a religiously motivated military campaign, their object the liberation of the Holy Sepulcher. The unexpected outcome was the adoption by the Christian West of some of the great achievements of Arabic civilization. This Arabic influence was to have an enormous impact on the further development of Europe, comparable in a sense to the influence of Hellenistic culture on the agrarian republic that was Rome. One can speak of a prelude to, almost an anticipation of, the Renaissance by three centuries. Europe is indebted to Arabic civilization not only for its numerical system, which made possible bookkeeping and, as a consequence, modern forms of capitalist organization; and for the astronomical and nautical knowledge that first made possible the great voyages of discovery in the fifteenth and sixteenth centuries. Its direct and obvious effect upon medieval Europe was in the luxuries that ushered in an entirely new way of life. And many of these new items even brought along their original Arabic names to the West. The carpet, the sofa, and the baldachin, with which previously bare and uncomfortable living quarters were now furnished, were Arabic, as were silk, velvet, damask, and taffeta, in which the upper classes now dressed—in contradistinction to the coarse linen of their subjects. Essentially it can be described as a full-scale refurbishing of the life of the upper classes: they dressed in new materials, refurnished residential quarters in the new style, and even "disguised" the native foods with oriental seasonings.

The historically significant aspect of all this is that all the materials for these new vestments were imported. It would be accurate to speak of a borrowed culture. As a consequence, the Occident became substantially dependent upon the Orient as supplier—a situation comparable to that of twentieth-century European dependence on Arab oil. Just as oil is a vital raw material for the energy supply of industrialized countries, in the Middle Ages oriental luxury goods were indispensable to the lifestyle of the European upper classes. In both instances the Occident depends upon the Orient as its supplier, without whom it cannot function. Modern life cannot maintain itself without oil, any more than medieval civilization could have been what it was without pepper, silk, and velvet. This parallel sounds more far-fetched than it is. History has shown that the hunger for spices was capable of mobilizing forces very much as the present-day need for energy sources has done.

Significant as oriental luxury goods were to European *culture* of the Middle Ages, they were no less important to the medieval *economy*. Foreign trade that provided these luxury items was an economic enterprise on a grand scale. Economic historians agree unanimously that foreign trade was fundamentally spice trade. Spices, with pepper heading the list, were the most highly prized of all luxury goods. They played the same role, historians have noted, as cotton and tea did in English mercantilism of the nineteenth century. One can understand the true significance of pepper and the rest of the spices only when they are viewed in relation to the other luxury items; but it is also true that pepper, as the most important among them, served as a sort of spearhead for the entire Orient trade, and as such can be viewed as representative. Thus if the following discussion centers on pepper and its economic, cultural, and historical significance, keep in mind that it also applies to all the other luxury goods that were reaching Europe. Only on this basis can one speak of the historical role pepper played.

The spice trade was as lucrative an undertaking as it was complex and prone to dislocation. Pepper was first transported from the Molucca Islands and India to Syria and Egypt by Arab middlemen. There it was bought up by Italian, primarily Venetian, traders who shipped it across the Mediterranean to Italy. Venice became the chief transfer point in Europe. Its heyday closely coincided with the period when Europe consumed the greatest amount of pepper, from the twelfth century to the sixteenth. With the profits from the spice trade the Venetian wholesale merchants built their marble palaces. The splendid architecture of Venice, flamboyantly displaying its oriental influence, became a sort of monument to the spice trade and its accrued profits. Venice marks both the high point and the decline of the medieval spice trade.

Toward the end of the Middle Ages the demand for spices rose once more to unprecedented heights. The circle of consumers expanded as the nouveau-riche urban middle class imitated the nobility in their ostentatious display of luxury. More and more people desired sumptuous, exotic clothes and sharply seasoned dishes, and this change in taste signaled the end of the Middle Ages and the dawn of the modern age. Pepper sauce had become an integral part of middle-class cuisine.

The spice trade reached the limits of its resources, becoming increasingly unable to satisfy this heightened demand. Trade routes that had served for centuries seemed suddenly obsolete. Shipment of goods across the Indian Ocean to Egypt and Syria, transport across the Isthmus of Suez to Alexandria, the reloading and shipping to Venice, and finally the arduous route over the Alps to central and north European markets could no longer satisfy the great demand, to say nothing of the prohibitive prices that resulted. Added to these technical transportation problems were those of a broadly international and political nature. Once the Mamelukes came into power in Egypt and the Turks in Asia Minor, the free trade that had existed up to that point ceased for the most part. Although the caravan route from Suez to Alexandria was not immediately cut off, the new rulers imposed extremely high tariffs.

In the fifteenth century the combination of these three factors —increased demand, stagnant transportation technology, and spiraling customs duties—led to a thirtyfold rise in the price of pepper coming from India to Venice. Rising demand and a limited supply at ever-higher prices resulted in a crisis situation. And crisis engenders a feverish search for a solution. Great innovative forces come into play—whether early capitalism in the fifteenth century or late capitalism in the twentieth, whether the product in short supply happens to be spices or petroleum. The fifteenth-century equivalent of today's quest for alternative fuel sources was a less costly trade route to the lands where spices grew, a route that would at once steer clear of toll restrictions and permit the transport of larger quantities of goods. The answer was a sea route to India, which was perhaps *the* grand obsession of the fifteenth century. A whole generation of entrepreneurs and adventurers went in search of this route. Christopher Columbus and Vasco da Gama were merely the successful heroes who made it into the history books. In any case, all who were caught up in this quest were driven by the prospect of the enormous riches that awaited the man who could put the pepper trade on a new, sounder footing. In the fifteenth century, control of the pepper trade meant having a hold over European taste and the vast sums that would be made available to maintain that taste. Whoever controlled pepper would essentially control the purse-strings of a continent. When the Portuguese, thanks to Vasco da Gama, succeeded in gaining a monopoly over the spice trade, they dictated prices as the Venetians had done before them. "The King of Portugal, Lord of Spices," as the Municipal Council of Nuremberg complains at the beginning of the sixteenth century, "has set . . . prices, just as he pleases, for pepper which, at any cost, no matter how dear, will not long go unsold to the Germans."

Thus the great voyages of exploration, the discovery of the New World, the beginning of the modern age, were all closely linked to the European hunger for pepper. This hunger became a driving force in history the moment obstacles arose to interfere with its satisfaction. The taste for pepper showed symptoms of having become an addiction. Once habituated to the spices of India, Europe was ready to do anything to gratify its craving. In the ensuing quest for a sea route to India, land of pepper, the discovery of the New World was, more or less, a by-product.*

Though the discovery of America was inadvertent, it proved soon enough to have an impact of the first magnitude on world history. The search for spices which led up to it offers a classic example of the Cunning of Reason. With the help of spices the Middle Ages were, so to speak, outwitted. Spices played a sort of catalytic role in the transition from the Middle Ages to modern times. They straddled the two periods, part of both, not quite belonging to either, yet decisively influencing both. In their cultural significance spices were wholly medieval; this is evident from the fact that they quickly lost that significance in the modern era. At the same time, they existed like foreign bodies in the medieval world, forerunners of the loosened boundaries of modern times. The medieval spice trade had already done away with narrow local borders. Like the money economy, the spice trade

---

* It would be rewarding at some point to investigate how long it took the Spanish to get over their disappointment at reaching not India but America, of not having landed in the land of pepper but in that of gold (El Dorado); and also to study how long the process of "reorientation," so to speak, lasted, whereby their lust for pepper was transformed into one for precious metals.

had entered the pores of the still-existing old order, already busily contributing to that society's dissolution. The hunger for spices, itself a specific medieval taste, was operating similarly. In its own way, still embedded in the religious conceptions of medieval Christianity, this taste crossed the old boundaries. A peculiarly medieval longing for faraway places—the longing we have seen for the Paradise they thought could be tasted in the spices. Paradise, in a mingling of the Christian and the exotic, was a fantastic world beyond local everyday life, not quite of this world nor of the other, located somewhere in the Orient. Something of this notion survives in the censer-swinging of the Catholic mass.

The modern era starts out in medieval guise with its quest for spices and for Paradise. The New World, discovered in the process, proved too vast, with a dynamic too much its own: "indigestible" for the Middle Ages. Thus spices lured the Old World into the New, where it lost its way. Nor would this historical background fail to leave traces on the New World. From the Spanish conquistadores to the propagandists for the American Way of Life, the New World has been hymned as a potential paradise. The paradise that the Middle Ages had sought became secularized as the land of unlimited possibilities.

The mediating role spices played between medieval and modern times is confirmed when we consider when they were at their peak. Between the eleventh and seventeenth centuries, that is, from the time of the Crusades to the period of the Dutch and English East India companies, spices dominated European taste. They were part of it and stamped it from the first stirrings of interest in lands beyond Europe to the conclusion of the conquest of the colonial world in the seventeenth century. Once there was nothing more worth mentioning to be discovered and conquered, and knowledge of the earth became common, spices apparently lost their tremendous attraction. After the discovery of the sea route to India, consumption once more rose sharply, only to taper off in time. In the seventeenth century, spices lost their supremacy in world trade. The market was saturated, if not glutted.

Highly seasoned dishes no longer appealed to the European palate. With the French leading the way, European cuisine had evolved to become very much like the one we know today, more moderate in its use of spices.

This long-term transformation in taste is one factor responsible for the decrease in the importance of spices in international trade. Another, related, reason was the emergence of a new group of flavorings, or rather luxury foods, that would appeal to the Europeans at the beginning of the seventeenth century: coffee, tea, chocolate, and sugar. Economically and culturally they took on the role spices had played, becoming the most important goods in foreign trade and the basis for a new structuring of European taste.

TWO

·————

Coffee
and the
Protestant
Ethic

————·————

$\mathcal{T}$oward the end of the sixteenth century, Leonhart Rauwolf, an Augsburg physician, traveled through the Near and Middle East. He noticed that the Turks and Arabs were consuming a hot, blackish beverage much as Europeans drank wine and beer. In his book *Journey to the Lands of the Orient*, published in 1582, Rauwolf wrote: "Among other things they have a good drink which they greatly esteem. They call it 'chaube': it is nearly as black as ink and helpful against stomach complaints. They drink it from earthenware and porcelain cups early in the morning, also in public places without any hesitation. But they take only small sips of it and then pass these cups around, for they are seated next to each other in a circle. To the water they add a berry the natives call 'bunnu' which, but for its size and color, resembles bay tree berries, surrounded by two thin hulls. This drink is very

129

Der Ander Thail

der Rayß/ Doctor Leonhart Rau-
wolffs/ in die Morgenlender : inn welchem
fürnemlich gehandlet wirt/ wie er von Halepo auß
weiter nach Bagadet, auff die alte namhaffte Statt
Babyloniam zügezogen/ was er darauff, vnder we=
gen weitter gesehen/ vnd was jhme im hin vnd wi=
der raysen/ zü wasser vnd land begegnet seye.
Mit kurtzer vermeldung deß hohen
Gebürges Libani, der frömbden
Gewächs/ vnd auch inn=
wonern desselbigen.

LEONHART RAUWOLF'S *JOURNEY TO THE LANDS OF THE ORIENT*
Title page of the second part of the 1582 travel account, in which,
along with other curiosities, the Augsburg physician describes coffee
—one of the first allusions to it in Europe.

common among them, so that one finds quite a few who serve it in the bazaar, as well as shopkeepers who sell the berries there."

It is difficult to determine precisely when coffee was introduced to Arabic culture. According to legend, Mohammed was cured of narcolepsy with coffee. There are indications in Arabic medical literature that coffee was used medicinally as early as the tenth century. But in the Islamic world, too, it became a popular beverage relatively late, certainly no earlier than the fifteenth century.

Although the dating may be vague, the *logic* of coffee drinking for Arabic-Islamic civilization is incontestable. As a nonalcoholic, nonintoxicating, indeed even sobering and mentally stimulating drink, it seemed to be tailor-made for a culture that forbade alcohol consumption and gave birth to modern mathematics. Arabic culture is dominated by abstraction more than any other culture in human history. Coffee has rightly been called the wine of Islam.

Until the seventeenth century, coffee remained a curiosity for Europeans, mentioned in accounts of journeys to the exotic lands of the Orient. They could not imagine consuming a hot, black, bitter-tasting drink—much less with pleasure. It reminded them too much of hot pitch, which was used in medieval times for battle and torture.

The situation changed around the middle of the seventeenth century. Suddenly a whole set of hitherto unknown exotic substances became fashionable. Together with chocolate, tea, and tobacco, coffee made its entrance upon the stage of European luxury culture. It appeared in several different places at once, then spread in a quasi-strategic pattern of encirclement: in the south it surfaced in the Levantine trade centers, Venice and Marseilles; in the north, in the transshipping ports of the new international trade, London and Amsterdam. From these bridgeheads it quickly conquered the hinterlands. Around 1650 coffee was virtually unknown in Europe, at most used as medication. By about 1700 it was firmly established as a beverage, not, of course,

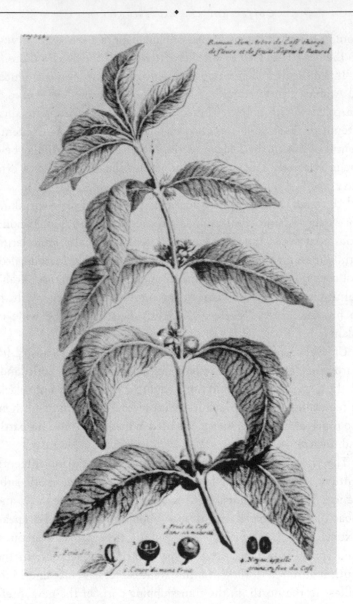

SPRIG OF COFFEE TREE WITH BERRIES

One of the earliest botanically exact illustrations, published in 1716 in
La Roque's Voyage de l'Arabie Heureuse, *one of the exotic travel*
accounts popular in that period.

for the entire population but certainly among the trend-setting strata of society.

Court aristocracy added coffee drinking as one more flourish to its cult of luxury. Coffee became as fashionable as the new chinoiserie, or the young blackamoor kept as a sort of mascot in one's retinue. Essentially it was not the drink itself that mattered to court society but how it could be consumed, the opportunities it afforded for display of elegance, grace, and high refinement. The porcelain that was created expressly for coffee drinking at the court was what mattered most—just as all aspects of life in an absolutist regime were determined by the forms of court ceremony. Form replaced content.

Bourgeois society of the same period regarded coffee in a different, quite contrary light. Not form, but substance—the drink —was the focus of interest. The thing itself, in this case, consisted in the actual physiological properties and effects ascribed to coffee. Were one to list all the properties they believed inherent in coffee, the result would be an amazingly motley catalogue of often mutually contradictory virtues. Here is just a small sampling: Coffee is good for colic, it fortifies the liver and the gall bladder, brings relief in cases of dropsy, purifies the blood, soothes the stomach, whets the appetite, but can also decrease it, keeps you awake, but can also induce sleep. It cools "hot" temperaments, but on the other hand it warms up "cold" ones, etc. Coffee, in other words, was viewed as a panacea. There wasn't a positive effect it was not credited with. If we wade through the jumble of properties most commonly imputed to it, however, we come up with two which are actually one and the same: sobriety and the power to sober up a person. In seventeenth- and eighteenth-century medical literature as well as in the general view, coffee was perceived as primarily a sober beverage, in contrast to previously known drinks, all of which were alcoholic. The late-seventeenth-century middle classes welcomed coffee as the great soberer. The coffee drinker's good sense and business efficiency were contrasted with the alcohol drinker's inebriation, incompe-

THE ARISTOCRACY'S FASHIONABLE BEVERAGES

Coffee, tea, and chocolate appealed to court society of the seventeenth and eighteenth centuries not only as exotic drinks, but also as occasions for self-display. The exquisite service and the young blackamoor who served it were basically more important to aristocratic taste than the items consumed. (Portrait of Madame Dubarry by Decreuse.)

DRINKING COFFEE "À LA TURQUE"

During the Rococo period, people loved to dress up and surround
themselves with objects in the oriental style. This masquerading
extended from Chinese porcelain rooms to little blackamoors serving
the beverages newly in vogue. As this engraving by Chodowiecki
shows, some even went so far as to dress up in "native" costumes to
drink their coffee.

tence, and laziness, most clearly in texts from seventeenth-century Puritan England. " 'Tis found already," wrote James Howell in 1660, "that this coffee drink hath caused a greater sobriety among the Nations. Whereas formerly Apprentices and clerks with others used to take their morning's draught of Ale, Beer, or Wine, which, by the dizziness they Cause in the Brain, made many unfit for business, they use now to play the Good-fellows in this wakeful and civil drink."

A Backward Glance: The Significance of Alcohol before the Seventeenth Century

It would be difficult for us nowadays to imagine the crucial role alcoholic drinks played before the hot, nonalcoholic beverages (coffee, tea, and chocolate) assumed their permanent place in the European diet. The former were consumed as both a semiluxury to be enjoyed and a nourishing staple. Medieval people drank copious amounts of wine and beer, especially on holidays—and holidays were quite numerous then (in Paris, for instance, 103 holidays were observed in the year 1660), including church consecrations, weddings, baptisms, burials, and "blue Mondays." On workdays beer and wine were a regular part of the meals.

Prior to the introduction of the potato, beer was second only to bread as the main source of nourishment for most central and north Europeans. "Some subsist more upon this drink than they do on food," wrote Johann Brettschneider, alias Placotomus, in the year 1551, referring not to hard-core drinkers, but to average folk: "People of both sexes and every age, the hale and the infirm alike require it." An English family in the latter half of the seventeenth century—the period when coffee drinking was catching on among the upper classes—consumed about three liters of beer per person daily, children included. Although large breweries already existed by then, beer brewing was still a part of housekeeping, like bread baking and slaughtering—one of the housewife's duties.

The best way to get a sense of how pervasive beer was in the seventeenth century, and often even in the eighteenth, is to remember that breakfast as a rule consisted of beer soup, a now-forgotten dish. In rural areas of Germany such soups were still prepared as late as the end of the eighteenth century. The following recipe—which already shows a considerable degree of refinement—comes from that period: "Heat the beer in a saucepan; in a separate small pot beat a couple of eggs. Add a chunk of butter to the hot beer. Stir in some cold beer to cool it, then pour over the eggs. Add a bit of salt, and finally mix all the ingredients together, whisking it well to keep it from curdling. Finally, cut up a roll, white bread, or other good bread, and pour the soup over it. You may also sweeten to taste with sugar."

How unusual the new hot beverages must have tasted to palates accustomed to the ubiquitous beer! The following passage from a letter written by Duchess Elisabeth Charlotte of Orléans illustrates this clearly. Of German origin, and more popularly known as Liselotte von der Pfalz, she complains about the taste of the three new drinks in fashion at the court of Versailles: "Tea makes me think of hay and dung, coffee of soot and lupine-seed, and chocolate is too sweet for me—it gives me a stomachache—I can't stand any of them. How much I would prefer a good *Kalteschale* [a cold soup, often prepared with wine and fruit—Trans.] or a good beer soup, that wouldn't give me a stomachache."

But it was the ritual function of alcohol, above and beyond its nutritional function, that explains what we now regard as the excessive consumption of alcohol in preindustrial societies. Drinking rites are of course still very much with us today. Drinking to someone's health, clinking glasses, the obligation to return another's toast, drinking as a pledge of friendship, drinking contests, etc.—these are rites and obligations one cannot easily evade. To earlier societies they were even more obligatory.

BEER AND HEALTH

Due to its nutritional value and low alcohol content, beer has been regulated since the dawn of history as the "good" alcohol, as opposed to stronger things like liquor. Where beer reigns, people are content, well nourished, and happy. What William Hogarth expressed for an entire society in his famous engraving Beer Street *(see p. 155) is similarly summed up by this portrait of a beer drinker by Martin Engelbrecht. The original text reads: "Balm to my breast as summer nears, / I do not quaff thee, noblest draught, / I sip thee, that my mind stay clear."*

Drinkers would work themselves into a state of intoxication that was not merely the result of the alcohol imbibed. It was also psychological in origin, fueled by the frenzy engendered in outdoing yourself offering toasts.

A drinking bout, once under way, usually ended only when its participants lost consciousness. To withdraw earlier was viewed either as an insult to one's drinking companions or as an admission of weakness on the part of the one who "chickened out." Observing a German drinking bout in the sixth century, the Roman author Venantius Fortunatus wrote that the participants "were carrying on like madmen, each competing in drinking to the other's health," and that "a man had to consider himself lucky to come away with his life." This essentially holds true also for the Middle Ages and for Germany up to the sixteenth century. Today competitive drinking to the point where participants lose consciousness is to be found in only a few social settings (rural weddings, Oktoberfest, student fraternities, etc.). It was a normal occurrence in the life of the preindustrial world.

One account of such a drinking contest in 1599 demonstrates how little things have changed in the thousand years between the Old Germanic society and that of the sixteenth century: "These drunkards are not satisfied with the wine they have in front of them, but contend with one another using drinking vessels as they would spears and weaponry. The foremost among them attacks, launching a round of drinks. Soon thereafter he bids those across the room to drink. Others are soon enlisted to join in on all sides with glasses and goblets. These guests and drunkards contend with each other, man to man, in pairs: they must swallow half, then all of a drink in one gulp, and without stopping to take a single breath, or wiping their beards, until they sink into a complete stupor. . . . And just as soon as two heroes emerge victorious, these men guzzle in competition with each other. And whoever is the winner and has best stood his ground carries off the prize. Sometimes the ones who drink the most are awarded honors and presented with trophies as well."

BEER BREWING
Until well into the nineteenth century, beer brewing, like slaughtering
and bread baking, was a part of housekeeping. The illustration by
George Cruikshank (top, facing page) shows one of these outdoor
home breweries. Comparing the dimensions of the casks with those in
the illustration of a brewery from the sixteenth century by Jörg
Amman (bottom, facing page), we see how little has changed over the
three centuries.

ALCOHOL AND THE MILITARY
Beer and, later, liquor were part of the regular food rations of
Europe's armies until the nineteenth century. From a 1632 decree by
Wallenstein (above) we see that a mercenary's daily ration consisted
of two pounds of bread, one pound of meat, and four pints of beer.
The inescapable presence of beer in military life is shown in an
illustration (next page) of a bivouac from around the end of the
sixteenth century: three huge barrels of beer fill the left third of the
picture.

THE TAVERN HOSTESS
Well into the seventeenth century beer was generally served by women, attesting to its domestic origins. In England particularly, "Ale Wives" became folklore figures—as in the case of Elinor Rummin, whose portrait appears on the title page of a book that Henry VIII's court poet, Skelton, dedicated to her in 1624 (top, facing page).

THE PORRIDGE EATER
In the painting by Jacob Jordaens (1593–1678) (bottom, facing page), the "porridge" is in fact probably beer soup. Before potatoes entered the European diet, this soup was a major source of daily nourishment. The massive, heavy body types that are seen in north European, especially Dutch, painting of the seventeenth century—and Jordaens's Porridge Eater *is one of them—have their nutritional and physiological explanation in the high beer and beer soup consumption.*

ELISABETH CHARLOTTE D'ORLÉANS

Also known as Liselotte von der Pfalz (1652—1722) and for her letters from Versailles to Germany, in which she complains of, among other fashionable innovations, the bad-tasting new beverages coffee, tea, and chocolate. (Painting by Hyazinth Rigaud.)

To be sure, there was increasing criticism of these drinking customs in the sixteenth century. The account just quoted, written by a Tübingen professor, Johann Georg Sigwart, is itself an expression of a new view of moderation articulated in a barrage of pamphlets, caricatures, sermons, and books. If the image this propaganda literature created were to be taken as literal truth, one would have to assume that sixteenth-century central Europe saw a sudden explosion of wanton drunkenness and gluttony. "When the city gates are closed, and those who live outside in the surrounding towns leave, they go weaving from side to side, stumbling and staggering, falling into the mud, their legs splayed out wide enough for a coach to pass through." Such descriptions should be taken with a grain of salt. They reflect not so much historical reality as opinion passed off as reality—which is to say that what changed in the sixteenth century was not actual alcohol consumption (which was already so huge that an increase was scarcely possible), but rather the attitude toward drinking.

This new attitude developed during the Reformation. Its chief representatives and advocates were the leading Reformers, above all Martin Luther. The Reformation, redefining the relationship between the individual and God as a *personal* one, at the same time took pains to regulate the relationship of man to alcohol. In so doing the Reformation was laying an essential foundation in both realms for the development of capitalism.

However, the movement to moderation in the Age of Reformation did not have especially lasting results. The numerous prohibitions against toasting rituals, intended to put an end to drinking contests, had to be repeatedly renewed, obviously having failed to achieve the desired effects. Nor were the apostles of moderation themselves the sort of thoroughgoing Puritans the Calvinist churches of seventeenth-century Holland and England were to bring forth. Medieval *joie de vivre* and the Protestant ethic were still inextricably joined in a person like Luther, who preached tirelessly against "Demon Alcohol" (a sixteenth-century descriptive term for alcoholism), yet who also coined

Vonn dem grewlichen laster
der trunckenheit / so in disen letsten zeiten erst
schier mit de Frantzosen auff komen / Was füllerey sauffen vn zütrin-
cken / für jamer vnd vnrath / schaden der seel vn des leibs / auch armůt
vnd schedlich not anricht / vnd mit sich bringt. Vnd wie dem
vbel zů raten wer / gruntlicher bericht vnd rathschlag /
auß götlicher geschrifft. Sebastian Franck.

Hüt euch das ewer hertz nit beschwert werd mit fressen vn sauffen /
vnd sorg der narung / vnd kom diser tag schnell vber euch. Luc. 21.

CARICATURES OF GLUTTONY AND DRUNKENNESS

*Following the Reformation, medieval eating and drinking customs
came under critical fire. A flood of polemical tracts, satires, and
caricatures, especially against immoderate drinking, was released.
The drunkard is usually portrayed as an animal, with the head of
an ape, a donkey, or a pig, and with bird claws and similar
appendages. Equally popular in these illustrations is the moment
when the imbiber "throws up." Frequently the scene is presided over
by "Demon Alcohol" (top, facing page), who was seen in those times
as both the cause and the incarnation of vice.*
Sequence of illustrations:
Frontispiece from Sebastian Franck's widely circulated diatribe On
the Abominable Vice of Drunkenness *(above).*
Title page from Matthäus Friedrich's Against Demon Alcohol *(top,
facing page).*
Hans Burgkmair: The Table of the Wealthy *(bottom, facing page).*
Title page from Thomas Heywood's Philocothonista, or, the
Drunkard *(top, p. 36).*
Title page of Dedekind's Grobianus *(bottom, p. 36).*

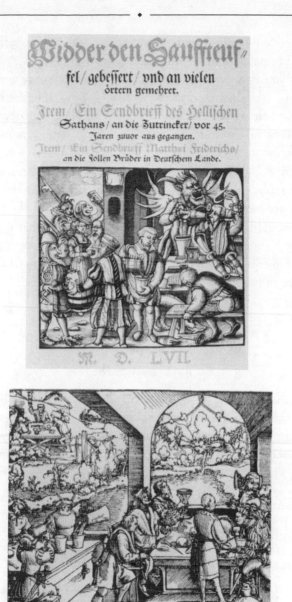

the proverb "wine, women, and song"—without which a man would remain a fool his whole life long.

Obviously conditions in the sixteenth century were not yet ripe for any real change in drinking habits. It would take not only Puritan ideology to condemn "Demon Alcohol," but some material basis to make it possible. That came with a more highly developed society and economy, sharper restraints, a higher degree of work discipline—and also a new group of beverages that could replace the old ones. For without substitutes the existing traditions would not disappear. Any substitute for the tried and true would have to have a new kind of appeal—that is, it must satisfy new needs—otherwise it would be unacceptable. These requirements were fulfilled by the new hot beverages that reached Europe in the seventeenth century—above all, coffee.

The Great Soberer

Coffee awakened a drowsing humanity from its alcoholic stupor to middle-class common sense and industry—so seventeenth-century coffee propaganda would have it. The English Puritan poets seized on this theme, as for example in the following anonymous poem published in 1674:

> When the sweet Poison of the Treacherous Grape
> Had acted on the world a general rape;
> Drowning our Reason and our souls
> In such deep seas of large o'erflowing bowls,
>
> . . . .
>
> When foggy Ale, leavying up mighty trains
> Of muddy vapours, had besieg'd our Brains,
> Then Heaven in Pity . . .
> First sent amongst us this All-healing Berry,
>
> . . . .

Coffee arrives, that grave and wholesome Liquor,
That heals the stomach, makes the genius quicker,
Relieves the memory, revives the sad,
And cheers the Spirits, without making mad . . .

Another two hundred years later the nineteenth-century poet-historian Jules Michelet would see coffee fulfill this historic mission as the sobering agent of an entire epoch: "Henceforth is the tavern dethroned, the monstrous tavern is dethroned, which even half a century earlier had sent youths wallowing 'twixt casks and wenches, is dethroned. Fewer liquor-drenched songs on the night air, fewer noblemen sprawled in the gutter . . . Coffee, the sober drink, the mighty nourishment of the brain, which unlike other spirits, heightens purity and lucidity; coffee, which clears the clouds of the imagination and their gloomy weight; which illumines the reality of things suddenly with the flash of truth . . ."

However, in the seventeenth century, coffee was not only considered a sober drink in contrast to alcoholic beverages, but above and beyond that it was credited with the ability to sober up people who were already drunk—a popular belief even today, in spite of all pharmacological evidence to the contrary. Sylvestre Dufour was the author-editor and compiler of a book on the new hot beverages. It had many editions and translations throughout Europe after its publication in 1671 *(Traitez Nouveau et curieux du café, du thé, et du chocolat)*. Dufour claimed to have seen the following episode: "Coffee sobers you up instantaneously, or in any event it sobers up those who are not fully intoxicated. One of my friends who had had too much wine sat down at the gambling table one evening after dinner. He was losing considerable sums, because having drunk too much wine, he was confusing hearts with diamonds. I took him aside and had him drink a cup of coffee, whereupon he returned to the game with a completely sober head and clear eye."

There was another series of attributes which the seventeenth century ascribed to coffee, none of them borne out by modern scientific findings. It seems that people of that era perceived coffee to have properties it could not possibly possess, but which they themselves projected onto it. A classic instance of the placebo effect?

If we examine another of these supposed properties, the motivation behind the projections becomes clearer. Michelet speaks in the passage that follows the section quoted above of "antierotic coffee, which at last replaces sexual arousal with stimulation of the intellect." What he had in mind here was the coffeehouse culture of the Enlightenment, the coffeehouse as the gathering place of intellectuals and center for discussion. In seventeenth-century England the idea of coffee as an antierotic drink was much more direct and concrete. It was regarded as a substance that reduced sexual energies, even to the point of impotence. It was recommended to clerics who lived in celibacy. In 1764 a broadside caused a great sensation in London. Its title: "The Women's Petition against Coffee, Representing to Publick Consideration the Grand Inconveniencies accruing to their SEX from the Excessive Use of that Drying, Enfeebling LIQUOR. Presented to the Right Honorable the Keepers of the Liberty of VENUS." The text expressed in no uncertain terms the fear that coffee would make "men [as] unfruitful as those deserts whence that unhappy berry is said to be brought." It is easy to identify the sociopolitical impulse behind this complaint: the English coffeehouses of this period excluded women, and in their pamphlet the women were rebelling against the increasing patriarchalization of society. That this opposition should use the argument that coffee makes men impotent shows, on the one hand, how powerful this notion was at the time, and on the other, how unpuritanical, indeed how antipuritanical, the women of this time were.

Coffee as the beverage of sobriety and coffee as the means of curbing the sexual urges—it is not hard to recognize the ideological forces behind this reorientation. Sobriety and abstinence have always been the battle cry of puritanical, ascetic movements. English Puritanism, and more generally, the Protestant ethic, defined coffee in this way and then wholeheartedly declared it their favorite drink.

There is no doubt that coffee is to a large degree an ideologically freighted drink. Yet it would be wrong to see only this aspect of it. For coffee undeniably has other properties that made it so well-suited to European civilization as it evolved from the seventeenth century on. Modern pharmacology confirms this. The caffeine in coffee affects the central nervous system. As a standard twentieth-century study states, it enhances "mental activity, speeds perception, and judgment at the same time that it makes them clearer, and it stimulates mental activity without leading to any subsequent depression." It is these properties that make coffee *the* beverage of the modern bourgeois age. The very point at which it was fully inserted into European culture confirms this. The seventeenth century was the century of rationalism, not only in philosophy, but in all the important areas of material life. The absolutist-bureaucratic state was built on the rationalistic viewpoint that originated in this period. Work in the newly burgeoning factories was organized rationalistically. Rationality and accountability characterize the bourgeois spirit that was behind it all.

The seventeenth-century bourgeois was distinguished from people of past centuries by his mental as well as his physical lifestyle. Medieval man did physical work, for the most part under the open sky. The middle-class man worked increasingly with his head, his workplace was the office, his working position was sedentary. The ideal that hovered before him was to function as uniformly and regularly as a clock. (The first example that comes to mind is the famous clocklike regularity of Kant, whose neighbors allegedly set their watches by his precisely timed daily walks.) It is perfectly obvious that this new way of life and work would affect the entire organism. In this connection coffee functioned as a historically significant drug. It spread through the body and achieved chemically and pharmacologically what rationalism and the Protestant ethic sought to fulfill spiritually and ideologically. With coffee, the principle of rationality entered human physiology, transforming it to conform with its own requirements. The result was a body which functioned in accord with the new demands—a rationalistic, middle-class, forward-looking body.

Arguments for and against Coffee

In the seventeenth century people judged the effect of coffee on the human body in various ways, depending on how they felt about progress in the first place. For optimistic middle-class progressives coffee's chief property, that of stimulating the mind and keeping one awake, was quite welcome. After all, it promised nothing less than to lengthen and intensify the *time* available for work. And inasmuch as time is money, to quote Benjamin Franklin, coffee indirectly proved to be a productive resource, or what we today might call a first-rate efficiency factor. In this sense, not to drink any coffee would be almost as great a sin for the puritanical bourgeois as wasting time itself.

This simple yet persuasive argument for coffee prevailed during the seventeenth and eighteenth centuries. However, at the same time, there were also different viewpoints, ranging from skeptical to explicitly hostile. Where such views were solely the expression of vested material interest (on the part of wine merchants, brewers, innkeepers, and groups representing their interests), they do not warrant our attention; but the criticisms of independent writers are quite another matter. Carl von Linné, or Carolus Linnaeus, the great eighteenth-century naturalist, for example, saw coffee's main virtue much as its advocates did, in its ability to keep people awake artificially. Yet he sees some problems, as the following sentence shows: "On this account [coffee]

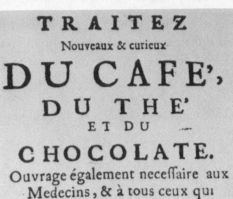

TRAITEZ
Nouveaux & curieux
DU CAFE',
DU THE'
ET DU
CHOCOLATE.

Ouvrage également necessaire aux
Medecins, & à tous ceux qui
aiment leur santé.

Par PHILIPPE SYLVESTRE DUFOUR

*A quoy on a adjouté dans cette Edition, la meil-
leure de toutes les methodes, qui manquoit
à ce Livre, pour composer*

L'EXCELLENT CHOCOLATE.

Par Mr. St. DISDIER.
Troisiéme Edition.

A LA HAYE,
Chez ADRIAN MOETJENS, Mar-
chand Libraire prez la Cour, à la
Libraire Françoise.

M. DC. XCIII.

TITLE PAGE AND FRONTISPIECE OF DUFOUR'S *TREATISE*
*Available from 1671 on in numerous editions and translations, this
book by a Lyon businessman, Sylvestre Dufour, became a sort of bible
of the new hot beverages. It was a compilation of many texts already
in wide circulation concerning coffee, tea, and chocolate. The
frontispiece shows the three drinks in the hands of figures
personifying their respective nationalities: on the left, the Turk or*

Arab with coffee (which was then still drunk, like tea, from a small handless bowl); center, the Chinese with tea; on the right, the Indian with chocolate. In front of them stand the appropriate containers, already in their familiar forms: the pear-shaped coffeepot; the wide, bulbous teapot; the slender, oval chocolate pot with its accompanying stirrer.

S. A. D. Tissot,

der Arzneykunst Doktor, und öffentlichen Lehrers in Lausanne, dann Mitglied zerschiedener Gesellschaften und Akademien,

von der

Gesundheit

der

Gelehrten,

und anderer Leute, die bey ihren Geschäff= ten wenige Bewegung machen.

Aus dem Französischen übersetzt.

Morbus est etiam aliquis per sapientiam mori. PLIN.

WIEN,
gedruckt bey Johann Thomas Edlen von Trattnern kaiserl. königl. Hofbuchdruckern und Buchhändlern.

1 7 7 0.

ON THE HEALTH OF SCHOLARS

The title—and especially the subtitle (And Others Who Get Little Exercise in the Course of Their Work)—*of this much-read book by the French physician Tissot is evidence of how a new lifestyle preoccupied people: the nonphysical activity, sitting in the office or studying all day. The century of the Enlightenment, which in its first half was interested only in the human mind, in its second half turned its attention to the problem of what effect this monopoly of mental activity would have on the rest of the body.*

might be considered useful by those who set a higher worth upon saving *their time than on maintaining their lives and health*, and who are compelled to work into the night" (author's italics). This already clearly shows an inkling, indeed a knowledge, of the price the body, or the health of human beings, must pay for progress in the form of greater concentration and labor efficiency. Linnaeus's remarks reflect a view that is related to Rousseau's ideal of nature and that is echoed in modern environmental consciousness: that it is our own ill-used, manipulated bodies that pay the price.

Half a century after Linnaeus, Samuel Hahnemann, the homeopath, paraphrased the same thought. Coffee creates an "artificially heightened sense of being," according to Hahnemann; "presence of mind, alertness, and empathy are all elevated more than in a healthy natural condition"; but, he goes on, these effects are unhealthy, in that they throw life off its natural rhythm, which consists in an alternation of wakefulness and sleepiness. It is worthwhile to hear out Hahnemann's argument against coffee more fully, because concisely and clearly it works out the problem raised by controlling the human organism with stimulants (and this in 1803):

"In the first moments or first quarter hour of waking, especially when waking occurs earlier than usual, probably everyone who does not live in an entirely primitive state of nature experiences an unpleasant sensation of less than fully roused consciousness, gloominess, a sluggishness and stiffness in the limbs; quick movements are difficult, and thinking is hard. But lo and behold, coffee dispels this natural but unpleasant feeling, this discomfort of mind and body, almost immediately. After a full day's work we must, by our nature, slacken and grow lazy; an unpleasant sensation of heaviness and fatigue in our mental and physical powers makes us cross and peevish, and compels us to seek the necessary rest and sleep. This peevishness and sluggishness, this unpleasant fatigue of mind and body with the natural approach of sleep, quickly vanishes with this medicinal drink; sleepiness vanishes, and an artificial sprightliness, a wakefulness wrested from Nature takes its place."

With Hahnemann we are entering the realm of modern medicine. If we now return to the period in which coffee was first discovered as a beverage, we find that the seventeenth and eighteenth centuries already had quite a similar awareness of the problem caused by the effects of coffee. However, it was formulated in medical concepts that no longer speak clearly to us and that therefore require some explanation. It is worth the trouble, for these old medical texts express ideas that strike us as both strange and familiar. Of course, their description of how coffee works does not hold up in light of today's scientific knowledge. But that isn't the issue. The documents should be read more as evidence of the contemporary attitude and awareness concerning coffee, attitudes from which we can deduce what coffee meant to people in those days. It is precisely the language, nonscientific by today's standards, the images and fantasies used, that give us a sense of the expectations, the conscious and unconscious fears, with which people regarded coffee. Let us begin with a passage from a paper delivered in 1679 before the Faculty of Medicine of the University of Marseilles. It describes the route coffee follows through the coffee drinker's body and the effects it has:

"The profuse burned particles it carries with it possess such a violent force that when they enter the bloodstream they sweep along all the lymph as well and drain the kidneys. Furthermore, they endanger the brain; after they have dried up its fluid and its convolutions, they keep all the pores of the body dilated and so impede the sleep-inducing animal forces from rising to the brain. Through these properties the ash contained in coffee induces such persistent wakefulness that the nerve fluid dries up; when it cannot be replaced, general prostration, paralysis, and impotence ensue. And because the blood, which has by this point grown as listless as a riverbed in midsummer, becomes acidic, all parts of the body are depleted of their fluid, [and] the entire body falls prey to the most frightful emaciation."

It is of secondary concern to us that coffee should be condemned in this medical expert's report. What matters are the notions, images, and ideas that are presented. The principal concept here is that a body will go to rack and ruin when its fluids are drained off. Coffee is viewed and condemned as a substance which drains and desiccates [vital] fluids. A healthy body, in this view of things, is a fluid-filled body; a sick body, one that is dry.

Judging well-being and illness by gauging the proportions of body fluids is a characteristic of the so-called humoral medicine that was popular in Europe in the seventeenth century and to some extent also in the eighteenth, despite the concurrent rise of modern medicine. Humoral medicine had its origin in the Greek and Arabic traditions, deriving its name from the Latin word for fluid or sap: *humor*. The present meaning of "humor" derives from this original sense of the word. Even into the eighteenth century "humor" did not necessarily refer to the comic, but quite generally to mood or state of mind. According to humoral medicine, a person's mood was the product of his body fluids. Here the classical doctrine of the temperaments even touches, or rather intersects classical medicine. Both are based on the so-called fourfold scheme *(Viererschema)*.

The fourfold scheme recognizes four body fluids which correspond to four temperaments and an equal number of properties. The body fluids are: blood, yellow bile, black bile, and phlegm. The temperaments are: sanguine, choleric, melancholic, and phlegmatic. The properties are: warm and moist, warm and dry, cold and dry, and cold and moist. In summary, that means for each combination of body fluid, temperament, and property, we get: blood, which is warm and moist, producing sanguine temperament; yellow bile, which is warm and dry, producing a choleric temperament; black bile, which is cold and dry, producing a melancholic temperament; phlegm, which is cold and moist, producing, of course, a phlegmatic temperament.

The fourfold scheme could be infinitely extended beyond body fluids and temperaments. It included calculations for the ordering of the heavens' cardinal points, for the seasons, designations for the ages of man, nutrition, and so on, which were each in turn assigned certain properties and linked to a particular temperament, body fluid, etc. In short, the fourfold scheme represents the attempt to create a universal medicine, to understand the human body in relation to and as a part of the entire nature of the world.

Not surprisingly, seventeenth-century medicine tried to fit coffee into this scheme. But there were obvious difficulties. Opinions varied as to whether coffee was a cold or warm, dry or moist substance, for its sobering and antisoporific effects were observed in equal measure among the different temperaments. Finally, its adherents agreed on the empty formula that coffee contained all the properties of the fourfold scheme, and it was therefore an appropriate remedy for the most varied temperaments: it cheered the melancholy, subdued the choleric, and animated the phlegmatic (the sanguine was held to be the "normal" healthy temperament).

At first glance, this canonization of coffee as panacea is quite meaningless. On closer inspection, however, we can glean from seventeenth- and eighteenth-century medical texts that coffee was thought to bear a special relationship to one of the body fluids, namely, mucus or phlegm, associated with the phlegmatic temperament. What we find in the negative evaluation quoted above turns up again and again in any number of other medical descriptions and, indeed, regardless of whether the author is arguing for or against coffee. It was generally thought in the seventeenth and eighteenth centuries that coffee dried out the body's phlegm and thereby robbed the phlegmatic temperament of its very foundation. Some examples are in order. Dufour wrote that coffee "dries up all cold and moist fluids." The eighteenth-century French physician Tissot wrote in his work *The Health of Scholars*: "Viscous phlegm, which lines the sides [i.e., of the stomach] is lost; the nerves are irritated, acquire a certain motility, and the vital forces fade away." The English physician Ben-

GROCERIES—GOODS FROM THE COLONIES
These so-called promotion slips (advertisements) of eighteenth-century London spice merchants show how the new semiluxury goods—coffee, tea, and chocolate along with sugar and tobacco—created an assortment of commodities unheard of only a century earlier.

jamin Moseley spoke of "coffee, which through its warmth and effectiveness, thins the mucous moistures, and improves circulation of the blood." Finally, Diderot's *Encyclopédie* emphasizes the especially benign effect coffee has on "heavy-bodied, stout, and strongly phlegm-congested persons," whereas it has a deleterious effect on those who are "thin and bilious."

To sum up: In the seventeenth and eighteenth centuries coffee was viewed as an extremely dry and desiccating substance. This view was surely associated with the actual roasting process coffee beans underwent, and which removed their natural moisture, their *fluids*. If, in one respect, the desiccation of the body through coffee was being assessed negatively and in another positively, one might well assume that a specific ideological position underlay each of these judgments. Let us anticipate a bit, and state outright that it was middle-class progressive writers who championed the draining of the body, and conservatives who viewed this same process as disastrous. This simple equation has a ready explanation.

In the seventeenth century anyone who regarded the mucus-rich body as the only healthy, fit type, necessarily was taking the phlegmatic temperament as the natural, God-given temperament. Remember, after all, that up until the introduction of the new warm beverages, beer was the basic source of nourishment in the diet (at least in England and Holland, the first middle-class nations). Beer, according to the nutritional science of the day, as well as simple direct observation, resulted in hefty bodies. Popularly beer and phlegm were mentioned in the same breath.

Although the seventeenth and eighteenth centuries viewed coffee as a drug that dried out the phlegm, the underlying reason was the actual replacement of beer by a new low-calorie—that is to say, nonfattening—beverage. This event in the history of nutrition translated into a specific new concept in medicine. The seventeenth-century writers who saw the phlegmatic, portly, *saftig* body type as the only natural one, and who considered any semblance of desiccation as fatal, must be called conservative because they thought the medieval diet the only one that was natural. The notion of dryness, which was then (and still is, in fact) associated with abstraction, nervousness, and so forth, offended the conservative sensibility. Dryness, however, is the modern principle par excellence. Dryness and sobriety are synonymous. Dryness is the principle of masculinity, patriarchy, asceticism, antisensuality, in contrast to the sensual and feminine. In this sense coffee is the great drying agent at the threshold of the modern age.

From the Coffeehouse to the Coffee Party

In 1687 or 1688—the exact date is not recorded—Edward Lloyd opened a coffeehouse on London's Tower Street. He named it after himself: Lloyd's Coffeehouse. Several years later he moved his operation, which had meanwhile grown successful, to Lombard Street, where it would remain in business for the next eighty years.

Lloyd's Coffeehouse soon evolved into a meeting place for people in the maritime occupations: ship captains, shipowners, merchants, insurance brokers. People went to Lloyd's to hear the latest trade news. From time to time, Lloyd himself ran a news service providing this sort of information, "Lloyd's News." This news-reporting venture flourished, its profits soon surpassing those derived from serving coffee. One sector of Lloyd's clientele in particular continued to expand—the insurance brokers. In the course of the eighteenth century Lloyd's completely shed its role as a coffeehouse and became the world-famous institution we know today, the largest insurance brokerage in the world.

This transformation began in the early eighteenth century when insurance agents would meet their clients in Lloyd's Coffeehouse to transact business. As the century advanced, the underwriters began to rent regular booths in Lloyd's, much as

LLOYD'S COFFEEHOUSE
Founded toward the end of the seventeenth century, it soon developed into the business hub of the maritime insurance trade. A century later "Lloyd's" itself became an insurance firm, moving into the Royal Exchange, but it also continued to function as a "normal" coffeehouse. The illustration above dates from this period.

brokers conduct their business in the stock exchange. When, at the end of the eighteenth century, Lloyd's actually moved to London's Royal Exchange, its transformation was complete. The former coffeehouse became the greatest insurance enterprise in the world when those insurance underwriters who had been its regular patrons decided to merge under a "constitution."

Not all coffeehouses that opened in London toward the end of the seventeenth century followed such a spectacular course. Lloyd's is the great exception. Yet its history epitomizes the role the coffeehouse played in the social and economic history of the early middle class as well as in its cultural history.

The coffeehouse of the seventeenth and eighteenth century has nothing to do with the modern *Konditerei*-café [pastry shop–café] —leaving aside the Viennese variety—except the principal drink it served. Its social, economic, and cultural role was almost the opposite of today's. Its clientele, far from being elderly ladies eating cake, were businessmen. In England women were denied access, though on the Continent they were tolerated. In other words, coffeehouses were primarily places to do business. Nor did the "business" have to be of an entirely commercial nature. In the seventeenth and eighteenth centuries, politics, art, and literature were also considered by the middle class to be part of business. In Vienna the coffeehouse continued longest as the site of these activities. In London, where the form first flourished, it also disappeared first, eclipsed in the eighteenth century by its successor, the club.

According to documents from the period, around 1700 there were some 3,000 coffeehouses in London. With a population of 600,000 that would have meant one coffeehouse for every 200 people. The number seems incredible. (Scarcely a century earlier, when beer was the unrivaled beverage of the people, the number of taverns had been around 1,000.) Exaggerated though the figure 3,000 may be, the fact remains that the coffeehouse played a central role during this period when London was the international hub of capitalism.

The coffeehouse as a public space was as novel as coffee was as a drink. As the name suggests, it was intended specifically to serve coffee. Although tea and chocolate were also available, that only underlined the establishment's nonalcoholic character. Sobriety and moderation were the order of the day for the coffeehouse: proper manners were required, talk was to be held to a subdued and considerate level—it was, in short, everything that taverns were not. The following "Rules and Orders of the Coffee House" date from 1674 and should give some idea of the coffeehouse code and character:

> *Enter sirs freely, But first if you please,*
> *Peruse our Civil-Orders, which are these.*
> *First, Gentry, Tradesmen, all are welcome hither,*
> *and may without affront sit down together:*
> *Pre-eminence of place, none here should mind,*
> *But take the next fit seat that he can find:*
> *Nor need any, if Finer Persons come,*
> *Rise up to assigne to them his room.*
>
> . . . .
>
> *He that shall any Quarrel here begin,*
> *Shall give each man a Dish t'atone the sin;*
> *And so shall he, whose Complements extend*
> *So far to drink in COFFEE to his friend;*
> *Let Noise of loud disputes be quite forborn,*
> *No Maudlin Lovers here in Corners mourn,*
> *But all be brisk, and talk, but not too much.*

On the basis of these rules the coffeehouse of the seventeenth and eighteenth centuries fulfilled its most important social role: as a center for communication. In a period that still had no daily newspaper in the modern sense, it functioned as a sort of news exchange. Lloyd's is an example of the coffeehouse serving as a commercial communication center. Yet the coffeehouse fulfilled this function not only for commerce. It was equally important for two other middle-class bourgeois activities: journalism and liter-

THE ENGLISH COFFEEHOUSE OF THE SEVENTEENTH CENTURY
*One of the earliest illustrations, a woodcut from 1674 (above), shows
an establishment as yet barely recognizable as a coffeehouse: the
guests sit at table as at an inn, and the innkeeper serves coffee out of a
jug that is in no way different from a beer, wine, or cider jug. Only
the drinking bowls—still without handles—show that these men are
not drinking beer or wine. Most remarkable is the calm, sober mood
that dominates the scene. One need only look at a corresponding
tavern scene from paintings of the same period to see the difference
and thus appreciate the contribution the coffeehouse made to modern
civilization. In the illustration of a coffeehouse on the next two pages,
the typical coffeehouse already becomes more recognizable by its
higher-class clientele in full-length wigs. The scene is dominated by an
item now typical of the coffeehouse, a sales counter, precursor of the
buffet, from which the hostess-cashier directs and oversees business.
This sales counter, not a feature of the traditional inn, derived from
shopkeeping, further proof that coffee had become a truly bourgeois
phenomenon.*

A·S 1663

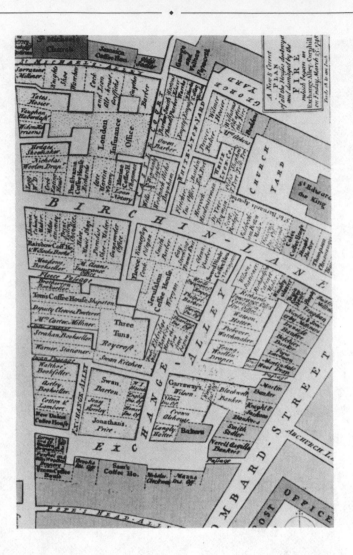

THE NUMBER OF COFFEEHOUSES IN LONDON

Documents from around 1700 cite the existence of some three thousand coffeehouses in England's capital. Even this later map from the mid eighteenth century gives an idea of their ubiquity in the city, although by this time, coffeehouses had to a great extent been replaced by private clubs.

ature. In the seventeenth and eighteenth centuries people frequented coffeehouses not only to conduct business but also to discuss political and literary topics—and to read the newspapers that were available there. The coffeehouse and newspapers, the coffeehouse and journalism, the coffeehouse and writers—these are old associations that would last into the twentieth century.

In the early eighteenth century the editors of London's weeklies used coffeehouses quite literally as their editorial offices. Richard Steele, the editor of *The Tatler*, gave its address as the coffeehouse the Grecian. He classified the various kinds of news according to which of the coffeehouses—news exchanges—had been the source of information, just as today news agencies are cited as the sources of newspaper stories; thus we read in the first issue of *The Tatler*: "All accounts of gallantry, pleasure, and entertainment, shall be under the article of White's Chocolate house; poetry, under that of Will's coffeehouse; learning, under the title of Grecian; foreign and domestic news, you will have from St James's coffeehouse; and what else I shall offer, on any other subject, shall be dated from my own apartment."

The connection between coffeehouses and literature is just as old as that between coffeehouses and journalism. For writers of the eighteenth century the coffeehouse was every bit the second home it was for journalists. The two professions, of course, were not as distinct then as they are today; indeed, they were often combined in a single writer, for example, Daniel Defoe, author of *Robinson Crusoe*. There was hardly a writer in the eighteenth century who did not frequent coffeehouses more or less regularly, at least in metropolitan London or Paris.

The most important direct effect coffeehouses had on literature was probably in helping to create a *culture of dialogue, of conversation*, which originated in coffeehouses and only then made its way into written literature. The prose of a Laurence Sterne or a Diderot, for instance, is conversational prose, a prose of dialogue, modeled, quite clearly, on coffeehouse discussion and "argumentation." The English literary historian Harold Routh describes

RICHARD STEELE (1672–1729)
Steele edited and published the weekly Tatler *in one of London's many
literary and political coffeehouses. (Portrait by Sir Godfrey Kneller,
1711.)*

the effect of this process on English literature as osmosis between reality and literature: "Until the time of the restoration, neither writers nor readers had practised the studied simplicity of true conversation. Even pamphleteers like Nashe, Dekker or Rowlands, whose one aim was to follow popular taste, had never broken away from book knowledge, despite their slipshod style, and the literary cliques which handed round manuscript essays and characters had reproduced in their writings only such conversation as might be a vehicle for their clichés and conceits. Men had confined their literary interest to the library and, as a consequence, their style was either ponderous or precious. The Royal Society had already started a movement against redundance of phrase; but it may well be doubted whether the protests of Sprat, Evelyn and South would have had lasting effect without the influence of coffeehouses. It was here that, besides practising benevolence in small things, men learnt to unravel literary ideas in a style that was colloquial as well as cultured."

The seventeenth-century coffeehouses influenced middle-class culture in so many and divers ways that it would be impossible to mention them all here. The coffeehouse exerted this influence in its role as a *social* center. It was *the* site for the public life of the eighteenth-century middle class, a place where the bourgeoisie developed new forms of commerce and culture.

In this respect the coffeehouse was comparable to two other institutions, the theater and the salon. The eighteenth-century theater—as a part of literature—represented an important locale for the self-definition of the bourgeoisie. This self-definition nevertheless remained on an aesthetic plane (however politically charged this may have been in the eighteenth century), while the coffeehouse was the focal point of life. In contrast to it the salon, which most closely approached the coffeehouse in its social function, was an aristocratic and elite institution. Entrée was limited to the intellectual giants of the bourgeoisie who had been invited by the aristocratic hostess, whereas anyone who could pay his tab could enter a coffeehouse. It would be intriguing to reconstruct

Café Politique

BREAKFAST BEFORE THE ERA OF WARM BEVERAGES
The still life Breakfast Table *by Willem Klaesz Heda (1594–1679)*
(above) shows the peculiar intermingling in the seventeenth century of
a still-medieval cuisine with modern refinement. The high standard of
culture is obvious from the elaborate goblets, the cake, and last but
not least, the presence of a pocket watch. Yet at the same time the
drink is still one that predates modern breakfast fare: wine. It was
only in the nineteenth century, after hot drinks were long established,
that dandies and snobs discovered champagne breakfasts and the petit
déjeuner à fourchette *["early lunch" or "late breakfast," forerunner*
of our modern "brunch"], i.e., breakfast without coffee.

PARIS COFFEEHOUSES, EARLY NINETEENTH CENTURY
Newspaper reading, chess playing, and discussion were the basic
activities here. German visitors to Paris were used to a much quieter
coffeehouse life. The actor and all-around theatrical figure Eduard
Devrient, for instance, marveled in 1839: "The way the gentlemen
come in, hat on head, cigar in mouth, and throw themselves down
stretching their feet out on the nearest chair, picking up any
newspaper, ordering brashly and loudly, all this was incomprehensible
behavior to me" (facing page).

the change in behavior of eighteenth-century Parisian intellectuals as they went directly from the salon of Madame De Deffand to the public Café de Procope.

But what did coffee itself have to do with these various influences exercised by the coffeehouses? Such influences obviously cannot be explained by the mere physiological effect of coffee, but only sociologically, i.e., sociohistorically. The coffeehouse functioned as a social setting, a place for communication and discussion, while the coffee served in it no longer played any discernible role. On the other hand, the coffeehouse owed its origin precisely to the serving of coffee. It owed its name, its very existence, to the beverage.

When coffee first reached Europe, the middle class drank it only in the coffeehouses. (The aristocratic forms of coffee drinking need not concern us here.) It took a half century—and in Germany almost a full century—for coffee to enter the domestic sphere, as a breakfast and afternoon drink. Thus it began its career in the public sphere, as a specifically *public drink*, and only later migrated into the private sphere to be served at home.

Here is a movement that follows all the typical stages in the history of innovations: some novelty fulfills its historical role—namely, to reshape reality in some crucial way—first in the public sphere, that is to say, in the sphere of collective consumption—and only later finds its way into the realm of private, domestic consumption. The public phase of an innovation can be termed *heroic*, in that it changes reality. The subsequent private phase must be termed *conformist*, in that, on its own, it demonstrates no change of dynamic, but functions rather to affirm and stabilize. Thus, for example, the transportation revolution in the nineteenth century began publicly, with the railroad as a means of mass transportation; in the twentieth century it took a private and domestic turn with the family automobile. Films began publicly with movie theaters; they then became privatized with the advent of the television set in the living room. In each instance what comes after is a *reduction*. It is not merely in scale or dimension that the machines in question are reduced when they move from the public sphere into domestic use—cars are smaller than locomotives, television sets smaller than movie screens—but the essential character of things is also diminished; the heroic aspect is lost, so to speak. In comparison with their tiny successors the railroad and cinema are powerful instruments that excite the imagination, inviting near mythical association. Cars and television lack this power and impact. They merely distribute or administer the reality which the earlier forms have created. The administrative and technological apparatuses, i.e., systems, that have made this diminution possible are in turn incomparably more monumental than their equivalents in the heroic beginnings; in some cases they may be highly visible (road networks), in other cases less visible (television).

This movement is discernible in the history of coffee as well. In its public, heroic phase, that of the coffeehouse, coffee was a powerful force for change, helping to forge a new reality. Moving into the middle-class home, to become a breakfast-time and afternoon drink, it grew passive, with a tendency toward the idyllic. It no longer exclusively symbolized the dynamic realm of early middle-class public life, politics, literature, and commerce; it stood more and more for domestic comfort, *Gemütlichkeit.*

However, we should distinguish between the two occasions for drinking coffee at home, breakfast time and in the afternoon. Breakfast coffee retained traces of the cultural-historical effects of the coffeehouse. It marked the start of the working day, formally putting an end to the night's rest, and making its drinkers alert and cheerful for the day ahead.

In the nineteenth century the daily morning newspaper was added to the breakfast ritual, yet another émigré from the coffeehouse. Remember that breakfast coffee now replaced the beer soup of earlier times, offering a domestic analogy to the supplanting of beer taverns by coffeehouses.

These functions and symbolic meanings were not inherent in afternoon coffee-drinking, known in Germany as the *Kaffee-*

THE MOTIF OF FAMILY COFFEE DRINKING

After its first "public" appearance in coffeehouses, coffee made its way during the eighteenth century into the private life of the middle-class family, in the form of breakfast or afternoon coffee. The family gathered around the coffee table (or tea table) now becomes a favorite motif for family portraits. Here is an interesting development: from formal portraiture to a realistic coffee scene.

In Jakob Denner's painting (1749) the family is arranged as in a traditional group portrait, the coffee table and service are random additions (above). In the rendering by an anonymous English master (top, facing page), we find a similar formal arrangement of figures, combined in a remarkable way, however, with a fairly technical interest in the coffee- (or tea-) drinking ritual itself: we see all the components of the service, and each person holds his cup in a different way, as though giving a demonstration of how to drink. Tischbein's painting (bottom, facing page) is similarly bound to the traditional format of the group portrait. Boucher's relatively early (1738) **Breakfast** *offers a more casually realistic scene (p. 66), of a sort even Germany's Biedermeier style was never to achieve, however highly it valued depictions of cozy scenes at the family coffee table, like those in the pictures by Jakob Milde (p. 67).*

LADIES' COFFEE PARTY IN THE EIGHTEENTH CENTURY
*A relatively rare theme in painting compared to that of families
gathered around the coffee table. (Abraham Schnapphuhn, Tea Party.)*

kränzchen, or "coffee party" (literally "coffee circle"). The coffee party was strictly a woman's affair; according to the definition in Amaranthes' *Frauenzimmerlexikon,* the "Woman's Lexicon," it is "a daily or weekly gathering of several closely acquainted women, each taking her turn as hostess, and in which the members divert and amuse themselves with drinking coffee and playing *Ombre.*" The dedication and ardor with which women would throw themselves into these ladies' coffee circles and coffee-drinking at home in general became a stock subject of comedies in eighteenth-century Germany, as evidenced by the playlets of the young Lessing, Gellert, or Picander. "It is well known," writes Picander, "that many a woman is so infatuated with coffee, that, if it were certain she would be served it in Purgatory, she would never care to reach Paradise."

It is obvious that this female passion for coffee is to be seen as compensation for women's exclusion from another, more public domain. Thus the afternoon coffee party functions as a sort of anticoffeehouse, a surrogate for the original coffeehouse created for male society. And yet the attempt to set up *Kaffeekränzchen* as domestic, feminine counterparts to men's coffeehouses lent itself to ridicule precisely because they became mere caricatures of their prototype. In the same way the Kaffeeklatsch or "ladies' gossip circle" became the butt of men's jokes in the eighteenth and nineteenth centuries, being viewed as a parodic debasement of coffeehouse talk. On the other hand, since the nineteenth century, men's coffeehouse talk has acquired more and more the traits of that domestic gossip the ladies shared over coffee. These developments converge finally in the twentieth century, as the days of gossipy literary cafés grow numbered, the male world abandons the coffeehouse, and the café is colonized by the ladies' circles—a belated revenge on the patriarchal coffeehouse culture.

CARICATURE OF THE COFFEE PARTY, NINETEENTH CENTURY

Coffee and Ideology

Just as the ladies' "coffee party" was a poor imitation of the coffeehouse, eighteenth-century German coffee drinking was a pale imitation of the English and French models. Provincialism, the lot of the German middle class ever since the Thirty Years' War, was evidenced even in the style and purpose with which coffee was drunk. Of course, there were coffeehouses in eighteenth-century Germany too, but they were hardly comparable with those of London and Paris. They had, as at least one observer noted, a markedly "philistine character." Perhaps in trading centers such as Hamburg and Leipzig they fulfilled social functions similar to those of the west European metropolitan centers, though here again on a smaller scale.

The "public-heroic" period of the coffeehouse in England and in France was skipped over in Germany, where right from the start coffee was limited to private, domestic consumption. In place of a coffeehouse ambience there prevailed the idyllic atmosphere, the "close intertwining of the new beverage with the coziness and comfort *Gemütlichkeit* of family life," according to cultural historian Paul Hoffman. Heinrich Voss's *Idylls* conveys this spirit most directly, as in the following poem, "Seventieth Birthday":

Mother would stand over the old stove, busily roasting the coffee,
In the heat that rose from the pan, she stood and stirred it round with wooden spoon;
The sweating beans crackled as they browned, while spicy and fragrant,
The aroma that rose from them spread through kitchen and hall.
Then she would fetch the coffee mill down off the mantelpiece,
Pour in the beans and, holding it tightly between her knees,

Her left hand keeping it steady, she would briskly crank the
handle.
Thrifty as ever, she'd gather up beans that strayed into her lap,
And then, finished, she'd pour the coarse-ground coffee onto the
grayish paper.

The idyllic treatment of coffee in the eighteenth century was in any event not the simple phenomenon it would seem to be at first sight. There was another, different motivation involved. The German relationship to coffee was an index of Germany's relationship to the advanced nations of the West. Coffee, in fact, would never have attained the eminent position it did in German middle-class life had it not already been a beverage that symbolized the power England and France had assumed in the world at that time. With coffee, the German middle class got to sample, as it were, a bit of Western urbanity it had not yet achieved for itself. The same mechanisms were at play as those that made English literature the supreme model for eighteenth-century German authors and that prompted Lessing, for instance, to give his heroines English names.

On the other hand, this German tendency to partake of world history by imitating certain symbolic forms of the western civilization from which it was excluded also entailed some alteration of these forms; they became germanized, at times beyond recognition. Thus coffee, which began as a symbol of public life, activity, business, etc., ended up as a symbol of family life and domestic tranquility.

The German relationship to coffee was further complicated by political-economic problems. These too were intimately tied to Germany's nonparticipation in world history, that is, world economy. For colonial powers such as England, Holland, and France, procuring coffee posed no problems. Until about the end of the seventeenth century they obtained their supplies directly from Arabia. When it became clear that the popularity of coffee would not be a passing phenomenon, that coffee had indeed become the daily beverage of increasingly broader sectors of the population, these nations began to produce it independently. The Dutch planted coffee in their East Indian possessions, particularly on the island of Java, as did the French in the Antilles. In this way they obeyed the fundamental principle of mercantilism, to import as few goods as possible, that is, to let as little money as possible flow out of one's own country. (The English chose a different path from the Dutch or French. They switched to another drink entirely: tea. But that is a separate topic, which we will be discussing further on.)

Germany, which had no colonies, had to satisfy its demand for coffee through imports procured through middlemen. In this way vast sums of money left the country. For the most part, they flowed into Dutch and French coffers, since the coffee plantations of the French and the Dutch produced not only to meet their own demands, but also for export to third nations, particularly Germany. Apparently this situation barely affected German coffee consumption in the first half of the eighteenth century. Things changed, however, after 1750. Coffee, together with a whole set of other imported items, came under the scrutiny of mercantile economic policies. Measures by the state to restrict coffee consumption followed: higher duties on coffee, state monopolies on its sale and roasting, and even outright prohibition of coffee.

The economic reasons for this new policy were not enough to make it acceptable to the population. It had to be cloaked in ideological, and in this case patriotic, garb. The coffee beans, hanging too high on the vine, economically, for Germany were thus declared to be "sour grapes." Coffee was declared an un-German drink, not merely because the flow of money out of Germany would make the country poorer, but also because the drink itself had supplanted Germany's hallowed national beverage, beer. A classically reactionary argument. We find it in the writings of authors such as Justus Möser and August Schlözer as well as in decrees against coffee like the following, issued in the bishopric of Hildesheim: "Men of Germany, your Fathers drank

THE GERMAN COFFEEHOUSE

In Germany the coffeehouse never had the social significance of its counterparts in London, Paris, or Vienna. Comparing the illustrations of Richter's Coffeehouse (above) and Classig's Coffeehouse (facing page) in Leipzig with the coffeehouse scenes from Paris (cf. p. 60), we see at once how different they were. While the Parisian cafés have the public quality of some portico-covered street, those in Leipzig look more like parlors into which the public has been admitted.

spirits, and like Frederick the Great himself were raised on beer, and were happy and cheerful. And this we too desire for ourselves. Send the wealthy half-brothers of our nation [the Dutch] money for wood and wine, if you will, but no more money for coffee. All [drinking] vessels, particularly cups and ordinary little bowls, all mills, roasting machines, in short, everything, to which the word 'coffee' can be prefixed, should be destroyed and smashed to bits, so that the memory of its destruction may be impressed upon our fellows."

The attempt to reduce coffee consumption through prohibitions and to return to beer was to remain an isolated episode. An entirely different development eventually led to the solution of the foreign exchange problem and at the same time to an acquired taste for a specifically German coffee flavor. This was the discovery of a coffee substitute, namely chicory coffee. The similarity in taste and color between chicory and coffee had been noted as far back as the eighteenth century. Twenty years later, at the height of active opposition to coffee, the hotelkeeper Christian Gottlieb Förster saw an occasion for trying out the coffee substitute. He applied for, and received, from the Prussian state of Frederick II, a six-year privilege to grow, process, and sell chicory coffee. The raison d'être of chicory coffee was graphically presented on the package in which it was sold. In the background we see an exotic landscape and a sailing ship carrying sacks of coffee, in the foreground a German peasant, sowing chicory and waving away the ship with a gesture of his hand. The caption reads, "Healthy and wealthy without you!"

Again it was not enough merely to point up the economic necessity of a coffee substitute and its lower price; rather chicory was depicted as a healthier choice than coffee. This was a later version of the old discussion about the relative wholesomeness of coffee, though in this case the ideological disguise is all too apparent. Ersatz coffee acquired a remarkable significance in the everyday psychology of the German petty bourgeoisie, which became its chief consumer. The earlier attempt to participate at least sym-

The young Goethe at the coffee table, as depicted in the late
nineteenth century by the painter Frank Kirchbach (b. 1859).

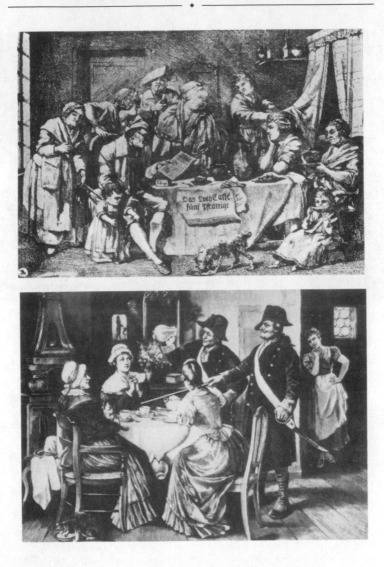

COFFEE TAXES AND COFFEE "SNIFFERS"
This etching by Johann Gottfried Schadow (1764–1850) (top) alludes to the Prussian tax on coffee, which put a stranglehold on imports in the latter half of the eighteenth century. The nineteenth-century painting The Coffee Sniffer *by Katzenstein (bottom) depicts a coffee raid by Prussian customs officers of the same period. These government agents were popularly known as "coffee sniffers."*

bolically in the lifestyle of the western nations (its obverse being a chauvinistic rejection of everything west European) was now given a further, certainly more intensely flawed expression.

The coffee drunk in Germany until about 1760 was the genuine article, imported from abroad. Chicory coffee was a sham, and self-deception. For no matter how hot, black, and coffeelike this beverage might look and taste, it was not the original—and no one could ever drink this ersatz coffee without such a conflicting awareness.

Real coffee was the aristocrat of coffee and the commoner's only-on-Sunday beverage, and as such was superior to ersatz coffee. The German petty bourgeois's social self-esteem and the esteem of others developed through the nose, as it were, through the aroma given off by the coffeepot: the family that drank genuine "bean coffee" assumed higher status than those who drank ersatz coffee. When finally post–World War II prosperity led to a democratization of real coffee, the once-important term "bean coffee" vanished from everyday speech, together with the lower middle class's heightened ability to discriminate between the smell of coffee and its substitutes.

England's Shift from Coffee to Tea

At the turn of the eighteenth century Great Britain was one of the major coffee consumers of Europe. Half a century later coffee played only a subordinate role. Tea had supplanted it. To put it statistically: in the period between 1650 and 1700 British tea imports totaled 181,545 pounds, in the next half-century 40 million pounds, more than a 200-fold increase. These numbers can only be regarded as approximations, of course. The statistics of the time comprised only those goods that passed through customs, not smuggled goods. Smuggling, though, was an important economic factor in the eighteenth century, and the smuggler was

TRACTAAT
Van het Excellenfte Kruyd
THEE:
't Welk vertoond het regte
gebruyk, en de grote kragten
van 't felve in Gefondheid, en
Siekten: Benevens een
KORT DISCOURS
OP
Het Leven, de Siekte, en de
Dood: mitsgaders op de Medi-
cijne, en de Medicijns van defe
tijd, en fpeciaal van ons Land.
Ten dienfte van die gene, die luft heb-
ben, om Langer, Gefonder, en Wijfer
te leven, als de meefte menfchen
nu in 't gemeen doen;
Door CORNELIS BONTEKOE
Doctor in de Medicijnen.

IN 'sGRAVENHAGE,

By PIETER HAGEN, Boekver-
kooper op de Hoogftraat, in de
Koning van Engeland. 1678.

TITLE PAGE FROM BONTEKOE'S TREATISE ON TEA

*The Dutch physician Cornelius Bontekoe, who practiced his profession
in Prussia, was, along with Sylvestre Dufour, the most tireless
champion of the new beverages in the seventeenth century. He was
especially taken with tea. "We recommend tea to the entire nation,
and to all peoples! We urge every man, every woman, to drink it
every day; if possible, every hour; beginning with ten cups a day and
subsequently increasing the dosage—as much as the stomach can take,
and the kidneys can secrete." Bontekoe recommended that the sick
take up to fifty cups a day! Contemporaries assumed he was paid for
these panegyrics by the Dutch East India Company, which dealt in tea.*

a significant social type: a socioeconomic renegade, challenging the power of the bureaucratic, absolutist state. Since the state imposed customs barriers on *luxury* goods, or *Genussmittel*, the smuggler came to be viewed as a sort of Robin Hood, defiantly helping the people to their enjoyment.

This supplanting of coffee by tea in England still remains an unexplained phenomenon. Surely neither a mysterious transformation in English taste—as has been proposed—nor some purely economic reason was responsible. It remains an unsolved yet fascinating problem in cultural and economic history. Its complexity is suggested here only by a couple of instances.

Like all European nations that began to drink coffee in the seventeenth century, the English at first also imported Arabian coffee. When it became clear that coffee was not going to be just a passing fad but rather an everyday institution, the various countries had their coffee supplied on a different basis. As we have seen, the French and the Dutch cultivated the coffee bean on plantations in their own colonies, to eliminate the flow of cash to Arabia.

In this light the substitution of tea for coffee seems England's own solution to the problem of foreign exchange payments. Yet when one considers where English tea came from, the riddle remains. It was not cultivated by the British themselves, but rather imported from China, which was still independent. Basically, then, the economic situation was identical to that of the coffee trade with Arabia, the sole differences being the trading partner and the article in question.

It would be beyond the scope of this book to trace the development of the English tea trade in the eighteenth century in order to come up with an explanation for the disappearance of coffee. This much can be said, however: the English tea trade was the monopoly of the East India Company, which has rightly been called a state within the state. The earlier coffee trade, on the other hand, was run by independent merchants. Translated into modern terms, the competition could be described as a contest

ENGLISH FIVE-O'CLOCK TEA AT THE BEGINNING OF
THE NINETEENTH CENTURY
(Drawing by Rowlandson, 1817.)

between a multinational concern and middle-class enterprises. It is quite obvious who got shortchanged in the process. The East India Company's position of strength was surely an essential factor in establishing tea on the English market and ultimately fixing it firmly in English taste even to this day. Yet other factors were in play too—for instance, the price ratio between coffee and tea.

A couple of price quotations will help to convey how hard it is to describe even this possible cause for the shift in taste with any precision: in London in 1662 a pound of coffee cost between 4 and 7 shillings. Around 1680 a pound of tea cost 11 to 12 shillings; at the beginning of the eighteenth century the cheaper varieties cost 8 to 10 shillings, the expensive ones 24 to 36 shillings. The price of tea thus continued to rise higher than the price of coffee. However, the price difference is more than compensated for by the smaller amount required to steep tea. Without knowing the strength of the tea and coffee brewed in the seventeenth and eighteenth centuries, we can assume from today's standards that an infusion of tea requires about a third or a fourth of the quantity required for coffee. Therefore, tea at the start of the eighteenth century was actually cheaper to use, even though more expensive to buy by absolute weight.

The shift from coffee to tea, whatever the deciding causes, may not have been drastically significant. It does not begin to compare, for instance, with the supplanting of medieval beverages by the new hot beverages. It is a matter of a change *within* a culture of consumption *[Genusskultur]* first revolutionized by coffee, not a major revision of the new historical plateau reached with coffee drinking. What the nineteenth century proved chemically, the seventeenth and eighteenth centuries felt, as it were, instinctively; namely that the very same stimulating substance (caffeine) was found in both tea and coffee. Tea also provided that central nervous system stimulation which mattered so much to the seventeenth and eighteenth centuries. An English text from 1660 describes the effect of tea as follows: "It makes the body active and alert. It offers relief against violent headaches and vertigo. It causes the disappearance of spleen. . . . It banishes tiredness and cleanses the vital fluids and the liver. It fortifies the stomach, improves digestion, and is especially apt for stout-bodied people as well as great eaters of meat. It is good against nightmares, it eases the brain and strengthens the memory. It is especially good for sustaining wakefulness. One infusion is sufficient to allow one to work through the night, without doing injury to one's body."

We see that the properties of tea are practically the same as those of coffee. The text just quoted is taken from one of the advertisements for the London coffeehouse Garway's, which like most coffeehouses of the period served tea as well as coffee. Even today, despite their different tastes, coffee and tea are considered in tandem, as part of the same family, and which of the two one prefers is practically a matter of "six of one, half a dozen of the other." This cannot be said of the third of the new exotic drinks introduced into Europe. Chocolate, pharmacologically as well as culturally, was quite distinct from coffee and tea.

THREE

·

Chocolate,
Catholicism,
Ancien Régime

·

Although coffee spread far and wide as the fashionable drink of the seventeenth and eighteenth centuries, it is still easy to determine its gravitational center: where capitalism and middle-class values had most thoroughly penetrated society: in the northwest of Europe—in England, Holland, and France. It was there that medical and literary writings were composed in celebration of the sobering and intellectually stimulating effects of the new beverage; there that the coffeehouse attained a social and economic significance unparalleled elsewhere; and there that coffee became *the* symbolic drink of the bourgeois order.

Much the same can be said of chocolate. At first glance, it too started as a generally fashionable beverage not limited to any particular country. Yet on closer inspection we realize that it too had its specific center of influence, one which lay in diametric

VENETIAN CHOCOLATE HOUSE

The "promotional slip"—as eighteenth-century business cards and similar forms of advertisement were known—depicts a cross between a shop and a public house. The goods are sold over the counter and also served at tables. (Cf. the coffeehouse counter in the illustration on p. 54.)

opposition to that of coffee—namely, southern Europe, Spain, and Italy, which is to say, in the Catholic world. If we label coffee a Protestant, northern drink, then chocolate must be designated as its Catholic, southern counterpart.

First, though, a word about the distinction between cocoa and chocolate. Cocoa is the name given to the plant and its fruit. Chocolate refers to the product known since the sixteenth century whose chief ingredient is cocoa. Like the substance itself, the name is of ancient Mexican origin. The ingredients from which chocolate is made vary according to taste. As a rule, cocoa, sugar, cinnamon, and vanilla are used. In the seventeenth and eighteenth centuries chocolate was sold in solid form, packaged in bars and cubes. It was consumed in liquid form, dissolved in hot water or milk, often with the addition of wine. Whenever chocolate is mentioned in the seventeenth and eighteenth centuries, it refers to this hot, liquid chocolate.

Chocolate was predestined to be the counterpart of coffee on the basis of its chemical composition. Cocoa, its main ingredient, contains no caffeine, but only a little theobromine, which is comparable to caffeine in its effect, though much weaker. Chocolate does not have a discernibly stimulating effect on the central nervous system—as medical writers in the seventeenth century were quick to note.

Even though chocolate does not have the stimulating effect of coffee and tea, it makes up for this by virtue of its great nutritional value. This is what made it so significant a commodity in the Catholic world. On the principle that liquids do not break fasts (*Liquidum non frangit jejunum*), chocolate could serve as a nutritional substitute during fasting periods, and naturally this made it a more or less vital beverage in Catholic Spain and Italy.

Yet this was only one aspect of its significance for the Catholic world. The discovery, trade, and consumption of chocolate were quite closely associated with His Most Catholic Majesty—as he was officially known then—the King of Spain. Once the Spaniards brought chocolate back to their homeland from Mexico at

THE ARISTOCRAT'S CHOCOLATE BREAKFAST

Not at the breakfast table, but preferably in bed, or at least in a
negligée or dressing gown—this is how the aristocracy in the ancien
régime liked to take its morning chocolate. Breakfast here does not
start off a workday; rather it marks the start of a day's carefully
cultivated idleness. The famous painting by Pietro Longhi (facing
page) gathers the breakfast participants, among them the obligatory
abbé and gallant, around the bed of the mistress of the house. In
Nicholas Lancret's painting (above), the bed has disappeared into the
background, yet the situation of the morning toilette, which the abbé
attends, is just as relaxed and informal as that in bed. The illustration
by Jean-Michel Moreau (next page) shows that the master of the
house includes chocolate drinking at his morning reception.

the start of the sixteenth century, it would remain an exclusively Spanish phenomenon for the next hundred years, thanks to Spain's monopoly on trade with the New World. (Beyond Spain it was known only in Spanish territories within Italy and the Netherlands.) It was in this century that it acquired its specifically Spanish identity, first as a clerical fasting drink and soon after as a fashionable secular beverage. At the court in Madrid it became a kind of status symbol. From there it inevitably became a standard feature of Spanish courtly style, which in the seventeenth century, in the days before Versailles, was the trend-setter for the rest of aristocratic Europe.

Toward the end of the seventeenth century the French style began to supplant the Spanish (having first assimilated its major elements). One important factor in this transitional period was the marriage of the Hapsburg princess Anna of Austria to Louis XIII in 1615. With Anna, who had grown up in Madrid, chocolate came to the French court; and here it managed to lose its Spanish, clerical aftertaste. It no longer carried associations of Jesuitical gloom, the Inquisition, and the Escorial; instead it simply represented Rococo elegance. It became the drink of the European aristocracy, as much a status symbol as the French language, the snuffbox, and the fan.

Aristocratic society preferred to drink its chocolate at breakfast. Ideally it was served in the boudoir, in bed if possible. Breakfast chocolate had little in common with the bourgeoisie's breakfast coffee. It was quite the opposite, and not only because the drinks were intrinsically different. Whereas the middle-class family sat erect at the breakfast table, with a sense of disciplined propriety, the essence of the chocolate ritual was fluid, lazy, languid motion. If coffee virtually shook drinkers awake for the workday that lay ahead, chocolate was meant to create an intermediary state between lying down and sitting up. Illustrations of the period nicely portray this ideal of an idle class's morning-long awakening to the rigors of studied leisure.

Morning chocolate in the boudoir was as popular a motif for

Rococo painting as pastoral landscapes and amorous bed scenes. Chocolate evidently appealed to the playful and erotic spirit of the age. Yet this association of chocolate and eroticism is not only iconographic in nature. According to an old belief that persisted into the nineteenth century, chocolate was an aphrodisiac. "People seek to be fortified through chocolate in order to perform certain duties," as a prudish end-of-the-seventeenth-century text euphemistically puts it.

Thus in this respect as well, chocolate appeared in the seventeenth and eighteenth centuries as coffee's opposite. The latter, as we have seen, was markedly anticorporeal and antierotic. Common wisdom had it that what coffee gave to the mind it took from the body. With chocolate it was exactly the reverse. It nourished one's body and one's potency; thus it represented the Baroque, Catholic acknowledgment of corporeal being as against Protestant asceticism.

The dichotomy was reflected in two types of drinking establishments in late seventeenth-century London. We have already had a look at the coffeehouse—above all, its bourgeois and puritanical character. Apparently, though, other establishments were set up to serve chocolate, the so-called chocolate parlors or chocolate houses. These were meeting places for an odd mixture of aristocracy and demimonde, what Marx would later refer to as the *bohème;* in any case, they were thoroughly antipuritanical, perhaps even bordello-like places.

Wherever we look in the seventeenth and eighteenth centuries, chocolate appears as the status beverage of the *ancien régime*, coffee as a stimulant for the ever more vigorously stirring bourgeois intellect and entrepreneurial spirit. Goethe, who used art as a means to lift himself out of his middle-class background into the aristocracy and who as member of a courtly society maintained a sense of aristocratic calm even in the midst of immense productivity, made a cult of chocolate, and avoided coffee. Balzac, who, despite his sentimental allegiance to the monarchy, lived and labored for the literary marketplace and for it alone, became one of the most excessive coffee-drinkers in history. Here we see two fundamentally different working styles and means of stimulation—fundamentally different psychologies and physiologies.

A final word about the fate of chocolate in the nineteenth and twentieth centuries. It vanished with the *ancien régime*. Or more precisely, it ended its existence as chocolate, continuing as cocoa, which has been drunk in its place since the nineteenth century. The modern cocoa process was developed around 1820 by the Dutchman Van Houten. Most of the oil from the cocoa bean is extracted; thus cocoa becomes less nourishing but far more digestible. In its new form it is a powder. This process put an end to the Spanish tradition of chocolate drinking, in which solid and liquid chocolate were identical. Ever since the nineteenth century the two have gone their separate ways. Cocoa now became a favorite drink in northern and central Europe too, but primarily for children. At the same time, the chocolate bar gained a new significance as a luxury in its own right. By an irony of history it was the two arch-Protestant countries that put an end to the Spanish, Catholic chocolate tradition. Holland became the first major producer of cocoa and solid chocolate in bar form, Switzerland following its lead with the innovation of milk chocolate.

Chocolate and cocoa are not common "adult" luxuries like coffee and tobacco. Cocoa became the preferred breakfast drink for children; chocolate and candy were given to women and children as presents. The former status drink of the *ancien régime* had sunk to the world of women and children. What formerly symbolized power and glory was now in the hands of those excluded from power and responsibility in middle-class society. Bourgeois society, as the historical victor over the old society, made a mockery of the status symbols once so important to the aristocracy. History repeatedly reveals how the self-esteem of the class that loses out is destroyed.

Other status symbols of the *ancien régime* shared this fate with chocolate: for instance, dress. Before 1789 an aristocrat's colorful, sumptuous costume was the expression of social prestige. His

CHOCOLATE AS APHRODISIAC
The original text that accompanies this illustration alludes to a view
widely held in the seventeenth and eighteenth centuries:
I bring to you a special drink from far across the West,
Although it's nearest loves on whom it's said to work the best.
Good cheer it always brings, and your full years renews.
First take a sip, my dear, and I shall presently;
and know I serve it to you with all the warmth that's due:
For we must take good care to leave descendants for posterity.

goal, if anything, was to present himself like a peacock; whereas for the simply dressed burgher nothing was more offensive and laughable than an association with this bird. Once again, in middle-class society it was children and women who were allowed to wear colorful dress.

What the peacock was for costume, the "sweet tooth" was in matters of gastronomic taste. The lover of sweets differed from the general gourmand or glutton. Middle-class taste, physiologically and by extension aesthetically, abhorred the bright and sweets, favoring somber black garments and bitter foods. In this sense coffee was both black and bitter, the antipode to the aristocracy's light, sweet chocolate—just as, in 1789 in Versailles, the Third Estate with its simple black garb was, politically and chromatically, diametrically opposed to the colorfully dressed aristocracy.

CHOCOLATE AS A CHILDREN'S DRINK
After centuries as an aristocratic beverage, in the nineteenth century chocolate became a nutritious morning drink for children. (French advertising poster, early twentieth century.)

FOUR

—— • ——

Tobacco:
The Dry
Inebriant

—— • ——

In 1627 the Palatinate's ambassador to the Netherlands, Johann Joachim von Rusdorff, reported on a new fashion there: "I cannot help but devote a few words to criticizing that new, astonishing fashion that came to our Europe some years ago from America, and which might be called a fog-drinking bout which outdoes all other passions for indulgence in drink, old or new. Dissolute persons have taken to imbibing and noisily drinking into their bodies the smoke of a plant they call nicotiana or tobacco, with incredible avidity and an inextinguishable zeal." Of all the pleasure goods that entered European civilization at the dawn of the modern age, tobacco is undoubtedly the most bizarre. It brought along completely new methods of consumption. In this respect coffee, tea, and chocolate were less revolutionary. The mere fact that they were drunk placed them in a continuum with the semiluxury goods known to Europe up to that time. As strange as their taste and their effects may have been, the *form* of their enjoyment was familiar.

For a long time there was simply no name for what you did with tobacco. Only in the course of the seventeenth century did "smoking" become a commonly used term. Up to that time it was compared with drinking—one spoke of "drinking smoke" and "drinking tobacco." Even in 1658 the Jesuit preacher and author Jakob Balde titled his satire against smoking "Die trockene Trunkenheit"—"Dry Drunkenness."

The analogy with drinking was thus at first a conceptual aid for grasping an otherwise bewildering novelty. Beyond that, however, the analogy was actually well grounded in the pharmacological effect of tobacco. Its main element, nicotine (named for the French ambassador to the Portuguese court, Jean Nicot, who brought tobacco to France around the mid sixteenth century), is more closely comparable in effect to alcohol than to caffeine. Nicotine does not stimulate the nervous system, but rather dulls it. Technically speaking, it is a nerve toxin. If a habitual smoker were to take in all at once the amount of nicotine that he consumed piecemeal in the course of one day, he would die from it. The comparison of tobacco with alcohol is also apt because of the thoroughly unpleasant effect newcomers to it experience. First attempts at smoking result in dizziness, queasiness or nausea, and sweating. As with alcohol, only after one gets used to it does smoking become a pleasure.

If in the seventeenth century smoking was interpreted as dry drinking, there was more in this than mere comparison of a strange form of pleasure to drinking. The quality of "dryness" makes for an underground link with another new pleasure item —coffee. As we have seen, seventeenth- and eighteenth-century medicine described coffee as a dry substance whose main property was to drain the body of its fluids. This concept was based upon the ancient medical schema of the four humors and the temperaments.

INDIAN WITH TOBACCO PIPE NEXT TO A TOBACCO PLANT
(Colored copper engraving, probably from the sixteenth century.)

SMOKING SCENES FROM THE ERA OF THE THIRTY YEARS' WAR
*This picture sequence appeared on numerous seventeenth-century
broadsides, while the accompanying text often changed. These same
illustrations of smoking might on one occasion serve as proof of its
salutary effects, on another the very opposite. The vomiting smokers
in picture H, for instance, are glossed as victims of tobacco, while
other commentaries describe this as an illustration of the effects of
tobacco abuse.*

CARICATURE AGAINST EXCESSIVE "TOBACCO DRINKING" CA. 1630
*Here it is no longer the thing itself but only its excesses that are
attacked. The three men seated at the table are obviously smoking
away contentedly; only the figure seated apart from them—with a
fool's cap and a gigantic pipe—demonstrates the dire consequences of
excessive smoking: his vomit is made up of symbols of folly: asses'
and rabbits' heads, and grasshoppers.*

FRONTISPIECE TO JAKOB BALDE'S "DRY DRUNKENNESS"
*Smoking as a fatal, unhealthy pleasure is represented in a way that
prefigures Hogarth's later depiction of the hazards of gin drinking (see
p. 154). Death, decay, and destruction dominate the picture. The
windowpanes are cracked, the cupboard door dangles on its hinge; the
skeleton in the foreground, out of whose empty eye sockets a (biblical)
snake rises with puffs of smoke, only too obviously illustrates the
author's idea of where smoking will lead. The link the title makes
between smoking and drinking—one much in keeping with the
prevailing attitude of the day—is illustrated by the figure vomiting in
the background. We see here how sixteenth-century representations of
drunkenness were perpetuated.*

Die Truckene Trunckenheit.

THE TALE OF SIR WALTER RALEIGH "ON FIRE"
*It is said that a servant of Raleigh's, on seeing his master smoking for
the first time, concluded that where there's smoke there's fire, and
assumed he was burning up from within. Flinging water over him, he
"put out" the blaze. The anecdote—here illustrated long afterward, in
1796—shows how bizarre smoking must have appeared to sixteenth-
and even seventeenth-century Europeans.*

Medicine of the seventeenth and eighteenth centuries viewed the effects of tobacco quite similarly. The similarities extended into the verbal formulations themselves. Like coffee, tobacco drained off one bodily fluid in particular, mucus. Thus we read in a pamphlet that promotes smoking, or rather "tobacco-drinking": "This tobacco-drinking . . . also removes the mucus and phlegmatic moisture; it is good for the dropsy, as can be deduced by the fact that this smoke removes moisture and makes the body thin and lean; and this smoke taken in by the body through tobacco pipes is a certain and excellent medicament against wheezing and shortness of the breath, against tuberculosis and lingering coughs, also against all persistent, thick, phlegmatic fluids and viscous elements." The antierotic effect ascribed to coffee also turned up again in medical descriptions of tobacco. A French treatise from 1700, *Le bon usage du Tabac en Poudre*, claims that tobacco "makes the brain and the nerves drier and steadier. This conduces to a sound faculty of judgment, a clearer, more circumspect faculty of reason and a greater constancy of soul. . . . At the same time, by virtue of this same desiccating effect, it weakens the erotic passions and steers the lascivious faculty of imagination, which takes hold over so many wanton men, in other directions."

As with coffee, this effect of desiccation and mucus depletion was viewed positively or negatively depending on the author's general outlook, and as in the disagreement over coffee, the line was drawn between bourgeois-progressive consciousness, which saw true health (i.e., productivity) in the antierotic desiccation of the body, and conservative opinion, which feared the destruction of the body (i.e., of the status quo) in any tampering with the natural balance of fluids.

Although the seventeenth century viewed the effects of coffee and tobacco in astonishingly similar terms, it did nonetheless note the great differences as well. If coffee makes a person wakeful, mentally alert, and, at worst, *nervous*, the effect of tobacco was described from the very first by reference to calm, placidity, con-

SMOKING AND CONTEMPLATION

This coupling of terms is found in all the literary and artistic
representations of smoking not fundamentally hostile to tobacco. As
in Ostade's village inn (facing page) or the portraits by Martin
Engelbrecht (above) and Johann Kupetzky (next page), smokers
always appeared as relaxed, meditative contemporary figures seated
often at writing desks, as lost in wreaths of pipe smoke as they were
in their own thoughts. The text accompanying the Engelbrecht says:
"Tobacco, when I smoke you, my mind soars to a state / of
wistfulness and reverence, and what I am I contemplate. / Smoke, an
untroubled haze, a gentle breeze, a shade: / The flesh's prop and stay:
a pipe of clay. / Who would not lift a glass your praise to sing / For
you are just as good as you are spiriting?"

templation, concentration, etc. The chemical basis of this effect is, as has been said, nicotine, which, in precise opposition to coffee's caffeine, does not stimulate, but rather tends to dull. Yet other factors also contribute to the calming effect of smoking. Added to the pharmacological are the factors of motoricity (the physical motions performed) and psychology. It is the combination of these elements that leads to the pleasure a modern medical writer (Kurt Pohlisch) describes in all its complexity: "The activity of smoking is formed by an extremely rich and variable concurrence of purposeful and expressive movements. . . . Already at the *motor* level and thus not merely as a result of nicotine, smoking abruptly relaxes conditions of psychomotor tension; it deflects irritation, nervousness into a calming motoricity. In the act of smoking the nervously restless hand fixes on a purpose. . . . Smoking creates both a feeling of activity in leisure and one of leisure in the midst of activity. . . . In terms of motoricity, pharmacology, and sense psychology, smoking creates a cheerful mood, highly varied nuances of physical feelings, an agreeable stimulation with which to perform intellectual work, a pleasant sense of calm, a state of contentedness, satisfaction [and] easy cordiality."

If one compares this description with texts from the seventeenth and eighteenth centuries, one finds their tenor much the same. Thus we are told in the following eighteenth-century text: "There is nothing better for contemplation than tobacco smoking, for here straying thoughts are recollected, this being most beneficial for students, in that while smoking they can grow accustomed to pondering everything well. Often enough one's faculties are divided, so that it is impossible to reason correctly over some difficult matter; among tobacco smokers, on the other hand, thoughts are collected, and afterwards too, although they rarely occur, weaknesses caused by overmuch zeal are dispelled. One remains calm within oneself and can make appropriate decisions about the most important matters."

Thus for authors in the seventeenth and eighteenth centuries,

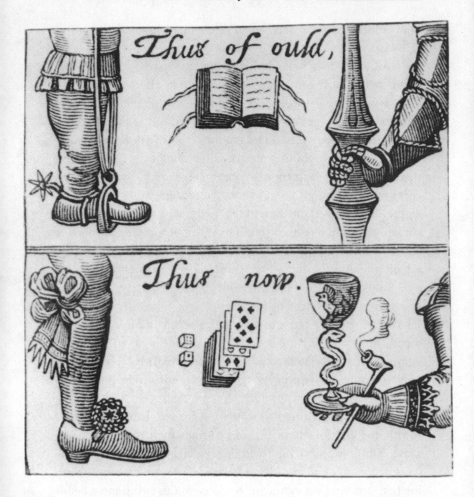

SMOKING AND DEGENERACY
Frontispiece from a 1627 pamphlet against smoking and drinking. The rider's spur-fitted leg turns into the decorative footwear of a cavalier; the book turns into dice and playing cards; the knight's lance-bearing arm turns into a cavalier's hand holding pipe and goblet.

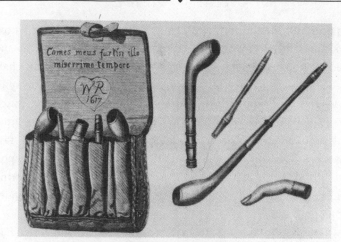

SIR WALTER RALEIGH'S SMOKING ARTICLES, 1617
*The Latin inscription on the inside of the case, "my companion in
those times of distress," refers to Raleigh's imprisonment.*

smoking and mental exertion are closely related. As the Dutch physician Cornelius Bontekoe (the proponent of coffee, tea, and tobacco) would have it, smoking is an activity which "can challenge and guard against all the adversity that a sedentary way of life is wont to bring with it." At about the same time the Dutch physician Beintema von Palma writes: "One who studies must needs smoke much tobacco, lest the spirits fade and falter, or start to work too slowly, in which event Reason loses its grasp upon especially difficult matters, and must be reawakened, so that the mind may receive all clearly and distinctly, well able to ponder and judge."

Although since the seventeenth century tobacco and coffee had been considered particularly suitable for the intellectually active, their effects stand in remarkable contrast to one another. Tobacco *calms*, coffee *stimulates*. Normally one would assume that these contradictory qualities cancel each other. Yet the opposite is true: they complement each other. The common goal both were used to achieve was the reorientation of the human organism to the primacy of mental labor. The brain is the part of the human body of greatest concern to bourgeois civilization. It alone was developed, cultivated, and cared for in the seventeenth and eighteenth centuries. The rest of the body, necessary evil that it was, merely served as a support for the head. Coffee and tobacco, each in its particular way, assisted this reorientation. Coffee functioned *positively*, arousing and nourishing the brain. Tobacco functioned *negatively*, calming the rest of the body—that is, reducing its motoricity to a minimum—as was necessary and desirable for mental, i.e., sedentary, activity. In smoking, the mentally active person works off those functionless, indeed dysfunctional bodily energies that had formerly been released in the physical work of prebourgeois man, in hunting, or in jousting. In this sense, smoking is an ersatz action. The fact that it is pleasurable changes nothing. The old instincts, pleasure and enjoyment, have apparently been pushed into retirement.

The Evolution of Smoking: Pipe, Cigar, Cigarette

If, from the seventeenth century to the present day, smoking has been universally characterized as a surrogate activity that calms, relaxes, and at the same time aids concentration, that holds of course only as a basic definition of smoking and its function in modern European times. In the last three centuries European culture has also established specific forms for smoking. The basic function—calming and concentration—has remained, but the forms—a succession of favored smoking implements—by which it is achieved have changed.

In the seventeenth and eighteenth centuries the pipe was the preferred smoking instrument. At the beginning of the nineteenth century the cigar appeared, and in the second half of the nineteenth century the cigarette—still the favorite of the three today.

If we look for some concept that adequately describes this evolution, what comes to mind is acceleration. Acceleration, of course, may well be *the* phenomenon of modern times. Industry produces an increasing number of commodities at increasingly short intervals, and people consume this rising stream of commodities with correspondingly greater rapidity and frequency. Since the sixteenth century everyone has experienced the speed-up of everyday life, be it in eating, dressing, traveling, working, or what have you.

In the history of tobacco use the act of smoking accelerates as the smoking process becomes simpler and shorter. Pipe smoking still needs an arsenal of equipment and manipulations before the pipe is ready to be smoked. A small, self-contained procedure is always necessary: cutting the tobacco leaves, filling the pipe, etc.

With the advent of the cigar at the beginning of the nineteenth century, this elaborate operation fell by the wayside. The product came fully prepared for consumption, needing only to be cut and placed in the mouth, an event that shortened and accelerated the

THE GRACE OF CIGARS

*From the moment feather-light, paper-wrapped cigarettes dominated
the scene, the cigar seemed a heavy thing, the symbol of a placid
conservatism. At the start of the nineteenth century, when it
supplanted the pipe, the cigar was considered decidedly graceful, light,
even feminine. "The pipe," we read in a text of this period, "is a
ponderous contraption that must be wielded in tranquility; the cigar is
easy to handle and does not hinder one's movement; the pipe smoker
is dull and domestic, the cigar smoker gay and lively in his
movements; the pipe is to the cigar as a lady in crinoline is to a naked
beauty." Finally, in the Germany of 1815 to 1848 cigars came to serve
as a sort of revolutionary emblem: Karl Marx smoked them. Only
later would they become a status symbol for entrepreneurs. Brecht's
cigar smoking thus was part of a nineteenth-century tradition. Our
illustrations are: lithograph (1825) after a painting by Sharp (facing
page), and French fashion plate from 1831 (above).*

ENGLISH CARICATURE OF THE CIGAR FAD, 1827

process, and was comparable to the later invention of the wooden match, which reduced the laborious process of striking up a spark to a single instantaneous gesture.

Half a century after the appearance of the cigar, the acceleration process advanced still further with the cigarette. Like the cigar, it came ready for consumption, yet the time required to finish smoking it was even briefer—quite a substantial innovation. The cigarette was light, short, and quick, in the physical as well as the temporal and pharmacological sense of the word. A "smoke," as this new informal unit of time is called, is as different from the time it takes to smoke a cigar as the velocity of a mail coach is from that of an automobile. The cigarette embodied a concept of time utterly different from that of the cigar. The calm and concentration a cigarette smoker feels in the twentieth century is quite different from that felt by the cigar or pipe smoker in the nineteenth century.

In the twentieth century, cigar and pipe smoking enjoy special status. They represent a definite intention not to conform to the prevailing mode of smoking, the cigarette. They deliberately flout convention, go against the prevailing rhythm of life, with an artificial time sense that suggests nostalgia, snob appeal, etc. Pipe and cigar smokers are as important, or rather unimportant, to an understanding of our era as are, say, antique car buffs; that is, they are interesting merely as a negative expression.

The standards of tranquility and concentration of a period can, in fact, always be deduced from the prevailing mode of smoking. They can even be quantified. The twentieth-century cigarette that takes five to seven minutes to be thoroughly smoked is meant to give all the leisure and concentration smokers in the nineteenth century derived from cigars that took almost a half hour to smoke. The new sense of time that each innovation in smoking embodies can best be felt when the traditional form of smoking is still in use. Thus at the start of the twentieth century the cigarette was a potent symbol of the new velocity of modern life precisely because the cigar was still ubiquitous. For the cultural historian

Alexander von Gleichen-Russwurm in 1914, the cigarette was "a symbol of modern life . . . which brings no peace, no sense of calm, no depth or reflection to serious conversation. It stimulates, but is extinguished as soon as the thought it has stimulated has caught fire. A casual distraction for idle hands, it . . . functions as the symbol of a hospitable home when time does not permit that anything else be offered."

As fast-paced, modern, and nervous as the cigarette appears in comparison with the smoking style of the pipe and cigar, the cigarette, in its own development, passed through specific stages of simplification, abbreviation, and acceleration. One example is the separate mouthpiece or tip. Today it is regarded at most as a quaint, nostalgic prop. In the early history of the cigarette, however, it was standard equipment for the smoker. Gleichen-Russwurm describes it, retrospectively, in 1914: "A predilection, now belonging to past fashion, was cultivated around the end of the nineteenth century for the cigarette tip, which was made chiefly out of amber and meerschaum. Simple in form and only rarely adorned with a crest or emblem, it constituted an important element of the smoking apparatus, and many a young man was proud of the fine, even, brown color the meerschaum acquired under his care. However, with more careful rolling and filling of the tobacco, the tip made of cardboard or gold paper gradually replaced the 'mouthpiece.' This was all the easier, since cigarette smokers probably had adopted it from a time when only pipes and cigars existed."

The cigarette case suffered a similar fate. It had long been an important item for the cigarette smoker. Cigarettes, which were bought singly or in plain packaging at a kiosk, were transferred to this artistically designed container—a time-consuming process whereby the individual converted an industrial mass-produced item to his own use, and one difficult to reconstruct today. In Europe the cigarette case disappeared only after the Second World War, in the wake of the Americans. Nowadays cigarettes are smoked straight from the commercial package.

SMOKING AND WAR: THE CIGARETTE
*Just as the Thirty Years' War contributed to the spread of smoking,
and the Napoleonic wars contributed more specifically to that of the
cigar throughout Europe, the Crimean War led to the expansion of the
—originally Russian—cigarette throughout Europe and, soon after,
the rest of the world. The lithograph by Marcelin depicts soldiers from
the Crimean War.*

MEN'S SMOKING PARTY WITH WOMAN
(Painting by Antony Palamadesz, called Staevertz; pp. 118–19.)

The Social and Spatial Expansion of Smoking

The same process that led from the pipe to the cigarette and to a more and more drastic simplification and acceleration of smoking led also to the advance of smoking into areas where it had previously been taboo, not only into specific places and settings but also a specific segment of the population—namely, women.

Like coffee, tobacco had long been a symbol of patriarchal society. Just as the early English coffeehouse was closed to women, women were also not allowed to smoke. Between the seventeenth and nineteenth centuries the woman smoker was the object of caricature. In the nineteenth century smoking acquired new symbolic significance for the emancipation movement. Rebels like George Sand and Lola Montez smoked quite deliberately in public. The right to smoke was demanded as much as the right to wear trousers. The forced humor of this newspaper article from the 1840s clearly shows how unsympathetically patriarchal society must have opposed this: "Women's emancipation takes remarkable strides forward in Germany, especially in Berlin, Germany's most discerning city, with the most startling results. In the brilliant circles of that city, girls aged nineteen or twenty speak confidently about Guizot, Thiers, and search laws—it all verges on the incredible! At this point many of these miniature George Sands don't even disdain the cigar; recently an elegant lady stopped a gentleman on the street who was smoking to ask him to light *hers*. Charming prospects, these! How long before they put on trousers, force men into the kitchen with riding whips, and nurse their babies on horseback! Easy for the emancipated woman! A public coffeehouse is already being opened for women, where debates on their status are to take place, together with cigar smoking, reading of the latest journals—all in all, the life of a gentleman. How happy Berlin husbands will be when they hold their cigar-smoking wives in their arms! In any case, to hell with them—may the devil take them!"

ROLE-SWAPPING: CARICATURE OF WOMAN SMOKER, EIGHTEENTH CENTURY

TOBACCO MANIA
(French caricature from 1842.)

Caricature by Grandville. Compare the role smoking women play here with the one they have in cigarette advertising half a century later.

LOLA MONTEZ WITH CIGARETTE

For feminist adventuresses like George Sand and Lola Montez, cigarette smoking was an important symbol for the image they wanted to project. After they met in Paris in the 1830s, George Sand adopted Lola Montez's habit of dressing in black, and Montez, Sand's habit of smoking. This photograph was taken around 1850 in the United States, where Montez ended her days.

It was at the end of the nineteenth century and clearly in connection with the first successes of the emancipation movement that women who smoked began to be socially accepted—as long as they smoked cigarettes. How tenacious traditional opinion is —even today pipe- or cigar-smoking women are regarded as eccentric and unfeminine. Cigarettes, on the other hand, were practically a symbol of femininity—not, admittedly, in the view of the feminist emancipation movement, but in general public awareness, most obviously in cigarette advertising. The shape and form of cigarettes contributed to this, of course; their lightness, their slenderness, the delicate white cigarette paper. "The cigarette belongs with champagne, games of chance and love, frivolity, sin, the poetry of pleasure," according to the associative effusiveness of a Viennese writer at the turn of the century, Paul von Schönthan; ". . . its aromatic, fleeting haze, vanishing in delicate rings and cloudlets, is the perfume of the boudoir."

Meanwhile, the cigarette discarded this feminine connotation much in the way it did the separate mouthpiece, which had been such a significant accessory in the smoking ritual. The mouthpiece or the unusually long cigarette holder turned women's cigarette smoking in the 1930s into an almost theatrical act. It would be tempting to interpret the oral-erotic element of this self-portrayal in terms of cultural history and psychoanalysis, as a typical expression of the period between 1890 and 1930.

The *social* expansion of smoking because of the cigarette coincided with a *spatial* expansion. Both movements of course are too intimately related to be neatly separated. As long as the smoking of pipes and cigars resulted in a strong accumulation of smoke and was the exclusive prerogative of men, it remained confined to certain spaces. Middle-class residences of the nineteenth century contained a room reserved for just this purpose, the smoking room or the study. Smoking was not permitted anywhere else. This held true especially for outdoor public places, where an explicit ban on smoking was in effect for a long time. Originally this was essentially justified by the danger of fire in cities built to

WOMEN AND CIGARETTES
Around the turn of the twentieth century, when the cigarette came into its own, the relation of women to smoking underwent an about-face. In the nineteenth century the woman smoker had been an object of caricature, while on the other hand the women's emancipation movement used smoking as a demonstrative symbol; now the cigarette appeared as a distinctly feminine prop. The illustrations: advertisement sketch from 1916 (above); fashion sketch, 1930 (facing page).

ENGLISH SMOKING CLUB, EIGHTEENTH CENTURY

*Before the cigarette became ubiquitous, smoking was confined to
certain areas. The reasons for this were social and practical. Smoking
was an exclusive privilege of men who wanted to remain among
themselves, and the accumulation of smoke from pipes was so heavy
it had to be confined to one room. Both reasons collapsed with the
advent of the cigarette. This picture by Robert Dighton of a club for
punch drinking and pipe smoking is modeled on Hogarth's*
Modern Midnight Conversation.

a large extent of wooden houses. When this no longer applied, the official prohibition against smoking in public places became a symbol of political oppression. Once the streets, squares, and parks were "liberated" for smoking, it assumed a symbolic character similar to that which it had had for the women's emancipation movement. In the list of political demands that emerged in Germany's *Vormärz* [the period between 1815 and 1848], smoking in public assumed an important place, particularly in Prussia; the authorities, conversely, regarded it as a sign of political recalcitrance. "Just as someone who wore a felt hat instead of the then fashionable top hat was suspected of harboring revolutionary ideas, every smoker seen on the street was suspected of being a dangerous democrat" (Corti). One fact contributing to the political significance of smoking, or more specifically of cigar smoking, since that was the form smoking then assumed, may have been that in this period the cigar rollers actually formed the militant avant-garde of the workers' movement. They organized the first and most radical union in Germany. Thus it was a curious twist in its symbolic history that the cigar should later have come to be a status symbol for capitalist entrepreneurs—an inversion of its original meaning comparable to the fate chocolate suffered in the nineteenth century.

In Prussia the ban on smoking in public places was repealed in 1848, many years after it had been in most other states in Europe. Since then smoking has not been subjected to spatial restrictions, except in places such as theaters, movie houses, or meeting rooms, where safety was a consideration. (The most recent tendencies to restrict smoking do not enter into the discussion here.)

The ubiquity of smoking is a clear index of the state of civilization. If smoking is defined as an ersatz act which absorbs the increasing nervousness of civilized man, affecting the body's chemistry as well as its motor function, then this penetration of our culture by smoking demonstrates to what depth the culture is permeated by nervousness.

EIGHTEENTH-CENTURY SNUFF MANIA
Frontispiece of Johann Heinrich Cohausen's book of 1720 Satyrical
Thoughts of Pica Nasi, or The Cravings of a Sensual Nose.

Snuff in the Eighteenth Century

Smoking was undoubtedly the most popular and frequent form of tobacco consumption. Yet there was a period in which it lost a degree of its importance. In the eighteenth century snuff became a major cultural phenomenon. "Today one takes snuff at court as well as in the city; princes, lofty lords, and the people all take snuff," read a treatise on *Le bon usage du Tabac en Poudre* from 1700. "It ranks among the favorite occupations of the noblest ladies, and the middle-class women who imitate them in everything follow them in this activity as well. It is the passion of prelates, abbés, and even monks. Despite papal prohibition, priests in Spain take snuff during the Mass. The snuffbox lies open before them on the altar."

In the *ancien régime* snuff had much the same sociocultural significance as chocolate. It also had originated in Spain and reached the peak of its cultural prestige in eighteenth-century French court life. From here it, like chocolate and the French language, caught on as a status symbol of the European upper class. In France, shortly before the Revolution, eleven-twelfths of all tobacco was consumed in the form of snuff. Only in England and Holland, bastions of the middle class, did smoking remain the preferred practice of the bourgeoisie and the petty nobility.

For the cultivated person of the Rococo period taking snuff became an important social ceremony; the style with which one handled a snuffbox became a means of self-presentation, of self-display, and of judging others. The proper way to take a pinch of snuff, and in particular the way to offer such a pinch, were taken very seriously and taught like dancing and fencing. Here is a description in an instruction manual from around 1750 of how to offer snuff in fourteen motions:

1. Pick up the snuffbox with the fingers of the left hand.
2. Place it into the correct position in the hand.

3. Tap the snuffbox with your finger.
4. Open the snuffbox.
5. Offer the snuffbox to the others in your company.
6. Take back the snuffbox.
7. Keep the snuffbox open all the while.
8. Make a pile of the tobacco in the snuffbox by tapping on the side of it with a finger.
9. Carefully take up the tobacco in the right hand.
10. Hold the tobacco for a moment between the fingers before bringing it up to the nose.
11. Bring the tobacco up to the nose.
12. Take in the snuff evenly with both nostrils, without making a grimace.
13. Sneeze, cough, expectorate.
14. Close the snuffbox.

Just as the gesture of snuff taking was an important expression of a person's self-stylization in the Rococo period, the snuffbox was a permanent feature of Rococo costume, on a level with the ornamental sword, the ornamental walking stick, and the fan; only now did the handkerchief also become an artistically fashioned decorative article. The cultivated Rococo man had a snuffbox appropriate to every suit he wore. Among the posthumous possessions of Count Heinrich Brühl, the director of the Meissen porcelain works, Boswell recorded over six hundred suits of clothing with an equal number of matching snuffboxes. Besides their use as containers for snuff tobacco, these boxes were valuable for the precious stones adorning them. They were among the most prized jeweled objects of the eighteenth century and thus were exchanged as gifts of state among royalty. A snuffbox that the king of Spain gave to the sister of Louis XIV was said to have had a value of 1.5 million livres.

By virtue of these associations the snuffbox became as much the mark of aristocracy of the ancien régime as the cigar became a status symbol for industrial capitalists. In the eighteenth cen-

SNUFF RITUAL: THE FULL-LENGTH PORTRAIT

The snuffbox, as noted, was an integral part of Rococo costume. How a person used it summed up his entire personality. Such had already been the case in the seventeenth century, as the portrait of a French chevalier from 1688 shows (above). In the eighteenth century this attitude was so prevalent that the snuffbox even turned up in official portraits like that of John Scrimgeour by Gainsborough (next page). The fashion lasted into the early nineteenth century (p. 135).

THE DRAMATIC ACT OF SNUFF TAKING: THE "PINCH"
*The three previous illustrations gave us a sense of what sort of
gestural code evolved for snuff taking in the seventeenth and
eighteenth centuries. In the following two (above and facing page) the
Rococo shows off the grace of its snuff rituals. The other illustrations
present actual snuff taking; in any event, these actually belong to the
period after Rococo snuff taking: some of its features are clearly
caricatured in the illustrations from the early nineteenth century
(pp. 138–39), most particularly in Grandville's* Variété des priseurs
(pp. 140–41).

ah, qu'il est bon !

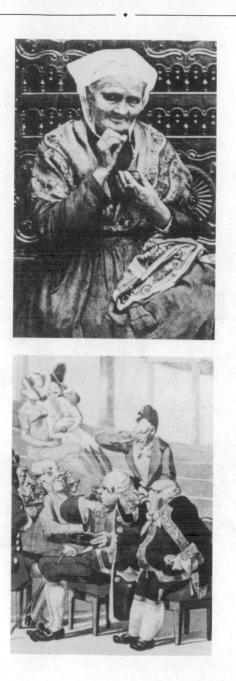

SNUFFBOXES IN THE ROCOCO
Among the most precious objects the eighteenth century produced,
they were ornamented not only by jewelers, but no less often by
galant *painters (facing page).*

la fille mal gardée

THE EXCHANGE OF SNUFFBOXES IN STERNE'S *SENTIMENTAL JOURNEY*
The brief scene at the start of the novel in which the narrator
exchanges his snuffbox with a monk stirred Rococo sentiment much in
the way Goethe's Werther *did. Many illustrations of the scene*
appeared, and clubs were started in which members exchanged
snuffboxes. This swapping became a symbol of fraternity.

tury the snuffbox represented exclusively the courtly gentleman's cult of pure luxury consumption. In Diderot's novel *Jacques the Fatalist* the snuffbox appears in surprising proximity to that symbol of bourgeois rationalization of time, the pocket watch. The theme of this novel is the relationship between master and servant, which would later inspire Hegel in his treatment of the master-slave dialectic. According to Diderot, there are three possessions that define a master: a servant, a watch, and a snuffbox. "He did not know," says Diderot of Jacques's master, "what to do without his watch, his snuffbox, or Jacques. These were the three mainstays of his life, the days of which he passed taking tobacco, checking the hour, and plying Jacques with questions."

Although the gestures and the social meaning of snuff taking differed a great deal from those of smoking, the eighteenth century regarded its physiological effect as identical. The desiccating and phlegm-depleting effect that was observed in smoking was found also in snuffed tobacco. The above-cited French text from 1700 described snuffed tobacco in the following terms: "If one takes a small portion into one's nose, it irritates the mucous membrane that fills the nasal cavity, as it does the nasal septum. It jolts it [the mucous membrane] into repeated contractions, whereby the small projections and glands that are distributed throughout are put under such duress that they discharge mucus —much like a sponge, when squeezed by a hand. Following upon this discharge comes a watery fluid from neighboring vessels and glands, according to the same principle whereby water issues out of a siphon."

In addition to this removal of mucus, snuff brought on another peculiar stimulatory effect. In the views of the eighteenth century the nose and the mucous membranes, like no other organ, represented a direct path to the brain. "There is no part of the human frame more delicately sensible than the nostrils," we read in an English essay of 1761 ("Cautions Against the Immoderate Use of Snuff"); "they are covered, in a manner, with branches of nerves: and these so thinly guarded from the air, *that the brain itself may be said to lie almost naked there."* The nose as the direct path—a sort of mouth—to the brain is a conception that naturally must have seemed ideally suited to this organ in a century of rationalism and enlightenment. The eighteenth century regarded the nose not as an organ of "basest" sense but rather as the organ of reason. That is why Diderot's *Encyclopédie* devoted an extensive article to the nose, in which it says, "The use of the nose and its mucous membranes demand the very greatest attention on the part of medical science." Even the eighteenth-century vogue for clean-shavenness, in particular the smoothly shaven upper lip, replacing the mustache and "handlebar" of the seventeenth century, has a partial historical and cultural justification. Snuff taking demanded a direct access to the nostrils unimpeded by facial hair.

The eighteenth century's interest in the nose as the instrument of reason also explains its indifference to one obvious logical consequence of snuff taking that by today's concepts would seem of far-reaching import. For the hyperstimulation of the mucous membranes through habitual snuff taking made the nose ultimately insensitive to smell, and in extreme cases fully robbed the user of this sense. Olfactory blindness due to snuff taking was one of the major illnesses of eighteenth-century civilized man. The opponents of snuff taking based their argument and their agitation on this fact. For members of courtly society, however, loss of the sense of smell was no catastrophe; on the contrary, it may have come as a relief. In the eighteenth century, people gradually became aware of the bad odors resulting from deficient personal hygiene and began to consider them an unpleasant odor. At first they tried hard to cover one smell with another. The eighteenth century witnessed the first boom in the perfume industry—less an expression of some new positive olfactory sensibility than an effort to escape the odors of the body. It must have come to people of that day as an altogether welcome side effect that together with its stimulating effect, snuff tobacco also managed to numb the sense of smell.

FIVE

·

The Industrial
Revolution,
Beer, and
Liquor

·

*I*n the 1840s the young Friedrich Engels reported from the industrial areas of England: "It is not surprising that the workers should drink heavily. Sheriff Alison asserts that 30,000 workers are drunk in Glasgow every Saturday night. And this is certainly no underestimate. . . . It is particularly on Saturday evenings that intoxication can be seen in all its bestiality, for it is then that the workers have just received their wages and go out for enjoyment at rather earlier hours than on other days of the week. On Saturday evenings the whole working class streams from the slums into the main streets of the towns. On such an evening in Manchester I have seldom gone home without seeing many drunkards staggering in the road or lying helpless in the gutter. On Sunday the same sort of things happen, but with less noisy disturbances. And when the revellers have no money left they go to the nearest pawnshop with whatever they have. . . . When we consider the vast extent of drunkenness among the English workers, Lord Ashley's assertion that the workers spend 25,000,000 pounds sterling a year on spiritous liquor can be readily accepted. It is easy to see the consequences of widespread drunkenness— the deterioration in personal circumstances, the catastrophic decline in health and morals, the breaking up of homes." If one compares this depiction of proletarian drunkenness in the nineteenth century with similar complaints from the sixteenth century, little enough seems to have changed. The texts agree down to their very wording. Again we have the vision of *drunkards reeling* and wallowing *in the gutter,* as distressing to observers of drunkenness in the age of the Reformation as in that of industrialization.

Are we to conclude from this that in these three centuries nothing had changed in the character, quality, quantity, or social import of drinking and drunkenness? Did people in the age of the Industrial Revolution still drink and get drunk in the same way, with the same motives, the same consequences, and the same drinks as people in the sixteenth century?

On the contrary, the success of the new beverages coffee, tea, and chocolate prove that in the interim a quite considerable shift in drinking mores had occurred. As we have seen, these hot beverages deprived alcohol of the status it had once enjoyed as the universal drink. Yet the sobriety they established was limited to specific sectors of the population, primarily the middle class. From the seventeenth century on, the bourgeoisie found unrestrained drinking increasingly offensive. Alcohol was not banned, of course, but it was domesticated. The middle-class citizen drank moderately, and he drank in a private circle (at home, in his club, or out amid a table of "regulars"). In Victorian England stopping in at a pub became almost as scandalous as visiting a brothel.

Things were quite different, however, for the lower classes. They had never had a share in the coffee culture of the seventeenth and eighteenth centuries. They remained bound to medieval custom in their drinking habits. Alcohol had an incomparably larger place in the lives of the proletariat than it did among the bourgeoisie. For the former, drink and drunkenness carried no social stigma; on the contrary, they were almost a symbol of class identity. In no other class did the archaic drinking rituals—toasting of drinking buddies, competing over how much you could hold, etc.—survive as vigorously as they did among the working class. Traces of these rituals can still be glimpsed today in workers' pubs. Yet it would be pure romanticism, that is, pure cynicism, to describe the role of alcohol among the proletariat as nothing but a survival of these archaic customs. Alongside the motive of drinking to symbolize social fellowship, there is another motive at least as important—escapism. Workers do not drink out of sheer exuberance; they drink to cast off the misery of their lives for a few hours. In every age, even in the Middle Ages, alcohol has to some extent been a "cure for cares," "for what ails." It would be a mistake to idealize the past by suggesting that before industrialization peasants drank solely out of *joie de vivre*, while later workers "drowned their sorrows" in drink. Both motives have always been a part of drinking.

Nevertheless, in the nineteenth century industrialization brought such an intensification of social misery into workers' lives that the motive of escapism became far stronger than it had been in earlier times. Friedrich Engels sketched the situation from which the individual working man sought momentarily to free himself through drink in the following words: "The worker comes home from his job tired and listless; he finds a residence that is without all comfort, dank, inhospitable and dirty; he urgently needs something to restore him, he must have *something* that compensates for his toil and makes the prospect of the next day tolerable; his tense, harried, hypochrondriacal mood, which is the product of unhealthy conditions, and which is a product in particular of indigestion, is exacerbated to the point of unendurability by his overall circumstances in life, the precariousness of his existence, his dependance on all manner of contingencies and

TRAGEDIES OF ALCOHOL

Pictorial narratives describing the ruinous path that led from the first swallow of gin to murder were very popular in nineteenth-century antialcohol propaganda. The illustrations shown here are taken from one such series: above, the youngest child has died due to the negligence of its alcoholic parents; top of facing page, the violent husband kills his wife; bottom of facing page, the husband goes mad at the sight of his wife's corpse.

his inability to introduce any degree of security into his own life; his weak body, enfeebled through bad air and bad nutrition, urgently demands some stimulus from without; his need for companionship can be satisfied only in a tavern, since he and his friends have no other place to meet—and all told, how is the worker not to have the strongest temptation towards inebriation, how could he possibly be in any state to resist the allures of drinks? On the contrary, it is a moral and physical necessity that under these circumstances a very great number of workers *must* succumb to drink."

Alcohol's new role as an escapist "cure for cares" was quite closely bound up with a new form of drink—distilled spirits. Among alcoholic beverages liquor was as modern as coffee was among nonalcoholic ones. It is certainly not a complete coincidence that both became important at approximately the same time. Liquor is the inverse of coffee, pharmacologically and socially. As such, it created new qualities of alcoholic inebriation, just as coffee created new qualities of sobriety. The polarity of these effects was reflected in the polarity of the two classes that adopted these drinks. Coffee was bourgeois, liquor proletarian.

Spiritous liquor had existed since the Middle Ages. Up until the sixteenth century, however, it had been used only as medicine. Apparently there existed no need as yet for a drink so high in alcoholic content. Beer still sufficed as a means of nutrition and intoxication for the lower classes. In the seventeenth century liquor became an everyday drink. As with so many innovations which later proved important for industrialization, liquor too found its first use in the military. It seems to have been a concomitant of the new discipline to which the military was subjected in the seventeenth century. The individual soldier who had previously been able to operate with relative autonomy became in the seventeenth and eighteenth centuries a cog in the wheel of a mathematically and rationalistically organized corps of troops. Liquor, which he received in his daily ration, served as a sort of physiological and psychological lubricant to guarantee his smooth functioning. The military's liquor allotments seem to have ensured the required measure of anaesthetization (that is, *not* intoxication) to make the soldier an integral member of the mechanical corps. Herein lay the rudiments of later industrial discipline.

Liquor dealt a deathblow to traditional drinking, which had been based on wine and beer. These might be termed *organic* alcoholic beverages, in that their alcoholic content is identical to the sugar content of the plants from which they are prepared. In liquor this relationship with nature was severed. Distillation raised the alcohol content far beyond the natural limits. To be precise, distilled spirits contained ten times the alcohol of traditional beer—which could not help but have far-reaching consequences. Whereas beer and wine are drunk slowly in long sips, and the inebriation process is gradual, liquor is *tossed off*, and intoxication is more or less instantaneous. Liquor thus represents a process of *acceleration* of intoxication, intrinsically related to other processes of acceleration in the modern age. The tenfold intensification of alcohol content over that of traditional beer meant that a person could now get drunk with one-tenth the quantity of liquor, or in one-tenth the time it had formerly taken. The maximized effect, the acceleration, and the reduced price made liquor a true child of the Industrial Revolution. It was to drinking what the mechanical weaver's loom was to weaving. The analogy can be further extended. The industrialization of drinking at first had as devastating an effect on the traditional lifestyle as industrialization had on the craft of weaving. In fact, liquor and the mechanical loom worked hand in hand, as it were, in eighteenth-century England, to destroy traditional ways of life and labor.

At the start of the eighteenth century beer was still the foremost beverage of the English people. Toward the middle of the century consumption of liquor, now called "gin," suddenly soared. From a half-million gallons (about 2 million liters) in 1684, production rose to over 5 million gallons in 1737, and to over 11 million by mid-century. With a population of roughly 6

HOGARTH'S *GIN LANE* AND *BEER STREET*
*This famous engraving depicting the world's ruin through liquor is a
comment upon the so-called epidemic of the eighteenth century.
Henry Fielding, the author and Hogarth's contemporary, wrote on
the same subject: "A new kind of drunkenness, unknown to our
ancestors, is lately sprung up amongst us, and which, if not put a stop
to, will infallibly destroy a great part of the inferior people. The
drunkenness I here intend is that acquired by the strongest
intoxicating liquors, and particulary by that poison called Gin [at the
time the generic term in English for all liquors]; which I have great*

reason to think is the principal sustenance (if it may be so called) of more than an hundred thousand people in this metropolis." While Gin Lane offers an image of destruction—collapsing houses, a dehumanized mother who drops her child, people assaulting one another, suicides, and only the pawnbroker's shop thriving—in its counterimage, Beer Street, peace, contentedness, and industriousness prevail. This contrast of beer and hard liquor survived into nineteenth- and twentieth-century discussions of the socialist movement, indeed to the present day.

million, that meant approximately eight liters of gin per capita. (By way of comparison: for the year 1974 West Germany's per capita liquor consumption was 2.6 liters, a bare third of England's in the eighteenth century.)

In the second half of the eighteenth century, gin consumption dropped to a more normal level. In this sense the so-called gin epidemic was a historical episode. But for that very reason it offered clear indications of the interconnection between the Industrial Revolution and the need for a cheap and powerful intoxicant.

Gin struck the typically beer-drinking English populace like a thunderbolt. Its social destructiveness was comparable to the effect whiskey later had upon the North American Indian cultures. The traditional drinking patterns could not cope with this highly concentrated inebriant. Drinking and intoxication totally lost their characteristic role of establishing social bonds or connections. Alcoholic inebriation gave way to alcoholic stupor. The eighteenth-century novelist and journalist Tobias Smollett has left us a direct record of the novel effect such strong spirits created: "Such a shameful degree of profligacy prevailed that the retailers of this poisonous compound set up painted boards in public, inviting people to be drunk for the small expense of one penny, assuring them that they might be dead drunk for two pence, and have straw for nothing. They accordingly provided cellars and places strewed with straw, to which they conveyed those wretches who were overwhelmed with intoxication. In these dismal caverns they lay until they recovered some use of their faculties, and then they had recourse to the same mischievous potion."

The gin epidemic has rightly been called a "social catastrophe of enormous proportions" (Monckton). Yet the drunkenness of the masses at this time merely reflected another social catastrophe. What was euphemistically termed "rural exodus," the "flight from the countryside," and in reality meant the expulsion of whole village populations from their indigenous soil through the so-called enclosures (another euphemism for expropriation by

THE GIN JUGGERNAUT
*Caricature by George Cruikshank, one of the most tireless crusaders
against alcoholism. From the beginning of the nineteenth century.*

THE GIN PALACE
Caricature by Cruikshank. Hogarth's motif of the mentally
incompetent alcoholic mother (see p. 154) is given a variant here in
the mother who gives her child liquor. The drinkers stand inside a
giant fox trap; Death stands by, ready to take them. The illustration
is of interest not only for its moral message. It is one of the earliest
pictures documenting the new mode of drinking while standing at the
bar. (See also pp. 200 and 201.)

large landowners) formed the background, or rather the breeding ground, for the gin epidemic. The uprooted masses poured into the cities. There they found themselves exposed to a frightening, alien world. All their traditional self-definition, the old norms and lifeways, had suddenly broken down. The result was utter disorientation.

Gin held out the promise to working-class people to help them forget their unbearable situation at least momentarily. It provided alcoholic stupefaction, not social intoxication. So began solitary drinking, a form of drinking limited to industrialized Europe and America. In every other age and civilization drinking had been collective.

Liquor has never lost the stigma of having been involved with this first brutal phase of the Industrial Revolution. It would henceforth be considered the vicious form of alcohol. Beer in contrast was the benign alcoholic beverage: it represented, so to speak, the golden age. It was viewed—as in the engravings of Hogarth—as a guarantee of happiness, contentment, health. The world of beer was all right; with liquor the world came apart at the seams.

But this was the predominant view even at a time when liquor did not yet represent a threat. Thus a petition to the English Parliament from 1673 reads: "Before brandy, which is now become common and sold in every little ale-house come into England in such quantities as it now doth, we drank good strong beer and ale, and all laborious people (which are for the greater part of the Kingdom) their bodies requiring after hard labor, some strong drink to refresh them, did therefore every morning and evening used to drink a pot of ale or a flagon of strong beer, which greatly helped the promotion of our own grain, and did them no great prejudice; it hindereth not their work, neither did it take away their senses, nor cost them much money, whereas the prohibition of brandy would . . . prevent the destruction of His Majesty's subjects many of whom have been killed by drinking thereof, it not agreeing with their constitution."

THE DRUNKARD'S PROGRESS
*A use of the old iconographic model of the ages of life applied to the
evolution of drinkers: in an ascending line it proceeds to maximum
enjoyment, then down into bodily and mental degradation and finally
suicide. (Mid-nineteenth century.)*

THE INEBRIOMETER
*A further example of how nineteenth-century antialcohol propaganda
sought graphically to pillory the advance or intensification of
drunkenness. The scale ranges from "temperate" to "dead drunk"
with small illustrations for each stage.*

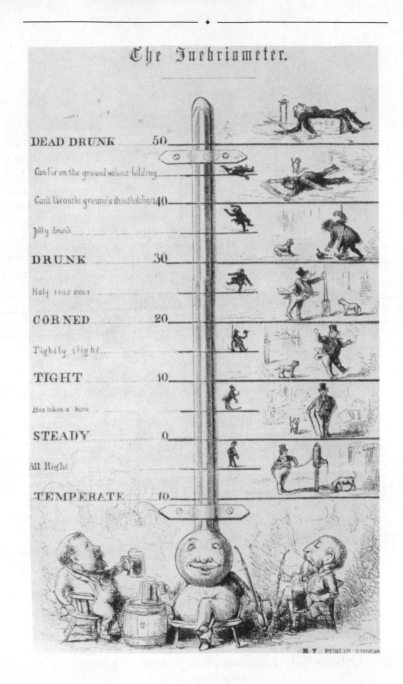

GIN AND WATER

A moral contrast in the manner of Hogarth's Gin Lane *and* Beer
Street. *The high Victorian representation of moderation goes far
beyond eighteenth-century ideas in that now beer too is condemned,
and thoroughly alcohol-free drinking demanded. With the rediscovery
of drinking water a new phase began, culminating in the United
States with Coca-Cola.*

WATER.

Contrasting beer with brandy in this way was of special significance for the organized labor movement in the nineteenth century, in relation to the so-called alcohol question. The alcohol
problem became a bone of contention in the socialist movement
of the nineteenth century. Discussions of how alcoholism in the
proletariat could most effectively be combated came down to two
distinct positions. One, coming from the puritanical Anglo-Saxon
tradition, called for total abstinence. The other considered moderate alcohol consumption—that is, beer—not only harmless but
actually beneficial. (Clearly the two sides represent a new version
of the Calvin-Luther opposition.) The Austrian socialist Viktor
Adler, a defender of abstinence, offers a fine insight into the
psychology of socialist self-discipline with his condemnation of
beer drinking, not on the grounds that it inebriates but because it
promotes comfort. In an article entitled "Down with Comfort
[Gemütlichkeit]!" he wrote: "We do not want to be comfortable;
as a matter of fact, our entire undertaking would benefit if workers were to experience a little more discomfort. We do not wish
to conceal anything from ourselves, but want rather to see clearly,
want to make ourselves better capable of work, more efficient,
and whereas compulsory labor can make use of other alcoholized
brains, work for the liberation of the working class requires clear-
sighted, cold-blooded people, it requires healthy brains." Elsewhere he insists even more emphatically on sobriety, rationality,
mental aptitude: "The revolutionizing of people's brains—that is
the hope, and the task of all those who are struggling for the
future of humanity."

Whereas for socialist teetotalers every drop of alcohol was a
threat to the existence of the workers' movement, the moderates
regarded only hard liquor as fatal. "Liquor—that is the enemy,"
was how Karl Kautsky formulated the alcohol politics of the social
democrats of the late nineteenth century. Wine and beer were
considered not merely a necessary evil, but physiologically and
even politically salutary. Engels in his descriptions of alcohol

abuse by the proletariat always proceeded from the assumption that liquor was the sole cause of the evil.

He even went so far as to draw a cautiously phrased analogy between alcoholic stupor and political mystification on the one hand, and wine and revolutionary wide-awakeness on the other. "I still remember quite well," he writes in the *Situation of the Working Classes*, "how at the end of the 'twenties the lowering in price of brandy suddenly reached the industrial region of the Lower Rhine. Particularly in that region and specifically in Elberfeld-Barmen, the mass of the working population succumbed to drink. . . . It is even open to question whether the dullness with which the north German workers in particular allowed the events of 1830 simply to ride right over them, without being moved in any way by them, was to a great extent due to brandy, which had more of an influence over them than ever. Serious and highly successful rebellions took place only in wine regions or in those German states that had more or less protected themselves from brandy through various tariffs. It would not be the first time brandy saved the Prussian State."

Not only did the consumption of wine and beer not harm the working class, but it was actually seen as a virtual necessity for their cohesion by Kautsky. In 1891, immediately after the repeal of the Socialist Laws, and in opposition to teetotalers like Viktor Adler, he declared: "For the proletarians such abstinence from alcohol means completely avoiding all social gatherings; the proletarian has no salon at his disposal, he cannot receive his friends and his companions in his parlor; if he wishes to get together with them, if he wishes to discuss with them common concerns, he *must* go to a tavern. Bourgeois politics can dispense with such an arrangement, but not proletarian politics." (Italics in original.)

When Kautsky conceded this political role to the tavern, what he had in mind was the situation in Germany under the laws enacted under pressure by the Socialists, when all official meeting places were closed and only the taverns were available as meeting places. But a look at the history of the European workers' movement shows that from the outset the public houses were of crucial practical importance. The first workers' associations in England, the so-called Friendly Societies and the Trade Unions, met in pubs. Members drank while they debated and debated while they drank. During strikes the workers' pub became a meeting place and communication center, as is true even today. In the nineteenth century the tavern was as important a place for the working class as the seventeenth- and eighteenth-century coffeehouse had been for the middle class. You might even say that the alcohol that was drunk here had a socio-pharmacological effect similar to that which coffee had had two centuries earlier. Alcohol and coffee each stimulated the qualities and abilities crucial to their respective classes. Just as coffee stimulates rationality, sobriety, and individualism, alcohol stimulates the proletarian virtues of collectivity and solidarity. Socialist teetotalers like Viktor Adler, who sought to deprive the worker of alcohol and tavern, were essentially trying to impose a bourgeois-puritanical model on the working class. They would have liked best to channel the proletariat through a giant coffeehouse. On the other hand, theoreticians like Engels and Kautsky saw clearly how deeply proletarian culture and mentality were anchored in alcohol and the life of the pub, and that there would be no class struggle without them, indeed that it could only be waged with them. "Without the tavern," says Kautsky, "the German proletariat has not only no social, but also no political, life."

SIX

— · —

Rituals

— · —

$\mathcal{T}$o visit a pub is to step into another world. For there the abstract law of exchange is suspended, at least in part. It's not that customers don't have to pay for drinks. The barkeeper is in business, after all. But somehow the rules of the outside world don't govern here.

Mass Observation, a sociological study undertaken in England in the 1930s, documents the drinking behavior of twentieth-century pubs and describes a typical scene. On a Sunday afternoon three men sit at a bar, each nursing a drink that he has paid for himself. A fourth man enters, and after ordering a drink and half-emptying his glass, he calls to the bartender to order drinks for all four. They begin a conversation, and after a while one of the other men orders another round. Two of the men who have not yet paid for a round are unemployed, but one of them orders the third round. When the drinks are placed before the group, the second of the two unemployed men leaves the pub, signaling his intent to return by leaving his glass half-empty. When he returns five minutes later, he finishes his drink and orders another four drinks. Now the round is complete. Later he confesses that he really did not want to be part of the round because he was short of money. He had to go home to get money because he felt he couldn't excuse himself from the round.

From personal experience everyone recognizes this unspoken obligation to participate in rounds of drinks regardless of whether he's in the mood or not, and even when he can't really afford it. Not to go along with it would be to lose face.

Yet this sort of obligation holds true only in bars, pubs, and saloons, and only in connection with alcoholic drinks. The idea of such a thing happening in a restaurant would be absurd. What is natural in a bar is meaningless on the outside.

Drinking, then, is apparently a special human activity, or, to quote from the *Handwörterbuch des deutschen Aberglaubens* [*Dictionary of German Superstition*], "the superstitious ideas and customs that center around the activity of drinking are to be understood as remnants of older magical, cultic actions and manifestations of belief."

But why should it be drinking to which these primordial notions have remained so strongly attached rather than eating, which is certainly as essential to life?

In the first place, archaic magical interpretations saw drinking and eating as equally conflicting processes. On the one hand, a person who consumes and incorporates things becomes their master. But on the other hand, he thereby delivers himself up to them, in a sense succumbs to them. For things have lives of their own. The plants and animals a person eats (aside from cannibalism) continue to have an effect within him, indeed work either *with* or *against* him, depending on whether they are well or ill disposed toward him.

What makes drinking more important than eating is the fact

that here the individual life or *soul* of a thing is being directly assimilated. In magical thinking every fluid symbolizes blood, and the blood or vital fluid of an animal or a plant *is* its soul. This accounts for the taboo against the presence of blood in food of most cultures, our own included. The Christian Eucharist still contains an echo of this identification of blood with the soul.

Because of this direct connection drinking had something menacing about it for primitive man. As he drinks, man assimilates the soul of something else and he loses his own soul in proportion to his drinking. Wine is the classical instance of this. The man intoxicated by wine no longer possesses his own soul, but is filled by that of the wine, that is, the wine god.

Like most magical conceptions, this one too has a grain of physiological truth to it. Liquid imbibed enters the bloodstream faster than solid foods. The effect for any given drink is more rapid, more immediately observable. And the custom of adding poison to drink has an actual physiological basis as well as the magical one. The poisoned drink is as old as mankind's drinking culture and drinking magic itself. In magical lore every drink is potentially poisoned or, to put it in more general terms, a threat, in that it might embody a soul hostile to the drinker.

Through history drinking rituals have evolved, aimed at neutralizing this menacing aspect. Drinking rituals are communal so that all will feel safe and be able to keep a watchful eye on one another. The king's taster, whose duty it was to test every drink set before his lord for poison, was a variant on this communal drinking, revealing its purpose explicitly.

The oldest and most important drinking ritual is the toast. In making their toasts the drinkers vow reciprocal friendship, goodwill, and good intentions, using traditional stock formulas. One such eleventh-century drinking oath goes: "Let the cups be brought and let us drink to health, drink after me and drink to me, drink to the full, drink half the cup and I shall drink to you." Another toast from the thirteenth century ran: "I drink to you, now drink as much as I do." In a sense, the drink itself was

A TOAST
(*Detail from a painting by Jan Steen,* The Family Feast.)

consecrated by these formulas, thus ceasing to be a threat. On the contrary, it became a guarantee and symbol of communality, friendship, and fraternity for those who were drinking. Toasting in archaic societies assumed proportions scarcely imaginable today. Even in the sixteenth century all drinking binges necessarily ended in the total inebriation of all participants, since it would have been an unheard-of breach of drinking etiquette for any member to quit sooner. In drinking etiquette it is taboo not to accept a proffered drink or, for that matter, not to reciprocate.

Communal drinking is, as has already been suggested here, characterized by a remarkable ambivalence. On the one hand, it creates fraternity among drinkers, on the other this relationship is marked by mutual caution, obligation, and competitiveness, which make it seem far less than friendly. In an instant the bond can be broken and turned into its opposite, should the basic rule be violated. Anyone who refuses a drink offered him in a workers' bar may well find himself in the middle of a brawl; if he does not in turn offer a round, he makes a fool of himself. Once he is a participant in a round of drinks, he cannot suddenly of his own accord back out. As the scene cited at the start of this chapter shows, he must observe certain rules, even if he is not in the mood. The American behavioral sociologist Sherri Cavan has determined from actual observation how ironclad these rules are, unwritten though they may be: "Once the proclamation is made that rounds have begun, it is incumbent upon the members of a group to participate regardless of individual preferences. One cannot demand that he pay for his own drink and his own drink only. If one of the members of the group must leave immediately after his first drink, he will usually state that he will stand the first round, being unavailable to stand any subsequent round. Although paying for more drinks than he will be consuming during the course of his stay may be economically unfair to him, it is required that either the other participants in the group accept his offer or that some other member volunteer to take the first round and allow the soon-to-be-departing member's drink to be defined as a gift drink. For example, if one member requests the first round because he must leave and his offer is declined, it is typically declined by someone saying, 'No, let me get the first round, and I'll treat you to a drink.' Once rounds have begun, each member of the group in turn is obligated to stand at least one round. Thus, if a group is composed of four members, rounds must continue for at least four drinks, after which another set of rounds may begin or the participants may begin purchasing their drinks on an individual basis. When rounds have started, the original group members typically remain together, at least until they have purchased their round, since each member of the group is obligated to purchase one round. Sometimes a member of the original group who has stood his round will move to some other part of the bar, but members of the original group who are yet to stand a round must still include him even though he is no longer physically part of the group. And he, in turn, must at least by gesture acknowledge each subsequent drink received from the group, thus maintaining social contact at least until the termination of the rounds.''

The above-mentioned study *Mass Observation* notes how far, indeed how deep into realms of the unconscious, the feeling of fraternity within a group of drinkers extends. Members of rounds will empty their glasses almost at the same time, and often the levels of the liquid in the glasses will vary by no more than half an inch. The variations are most marked when the glasses are less than half full. They begin at the same time and finish at the same, or almost the same, time. The study relates an impressive example of this telepathic sense of community by reporting about a group of four men of whom one is blind. All sit at a table and order their beer. As soon as the glasses are served, they all raise them to their lips and drink for about four seconds, each returning his glass to the table at the same time. Each, including the blind man, has emptied exactly a quarter of the glass. The next few times they drink in shorter gulps, sometimes the blind man first, sometimes the other three, without any noticeable pattern. But, at the end, they all finish their drinks with a variation of between a quarter and a half inch of beer remaining.

The rules and rituals that accompany drinking in a bar or pub survive in our modern civilization as relics from a long-forgotten age. The saloon or bar, in fact, may be termed a sort of *preserve*, in which archaic behavior patterns that have all but vanished from other spheres of life are kept alive. To fully understand the meaning of drinking rituals, one must recall these age-old modes of conduct, mechanisms, and rituals, and their social function.

This archaic practice which is perpetuated in drinking rituals is known in anthropology as a *potlatch*. The potlatch is a kind of sacrificial offering, not to the divinity, but to other human beings. In the potlatch valuable objects are either destroyed in the presence of members of another tribe (a destruction potlatch) or given to them (a gift potlatch). From a modern, rationalistic point of view this process seems senseless, but for primitive societies it has, as the French anthropologist and sociologist Marcel Mauss discovered, an absolutely central social importance: "The motive for these excessive gifts and this reckless consumption, the senseless loss and destruction of property is in no way unselfishly motivated. Among chieftains, vassals, and followers a hierarchy is established by means of these gifts. Giving is a way of demonstrating one's superiority, of showing that one is greater, that one stands higher . . .; to accept, without reciprocating or giving more in return, means subordinating oneself, becoming a vassal and follower, sinking deeper."

The potlatch creates an unstable social equilibrium. The tribes or chieftains who heap gifts on one another seemingly meet as friends on an equal footing, sealing their friendship with these gifts. In reality, though, a contest has begun within the medium of gift giving, a tourney of generosity. In the end, whoever does not—or cannot—reciprocate is forced to give up. Mauss goes on to comment: "One forever 'loses face' if one does not requite a gift or does not destroy something of corresponding worth. The penalty of obligation to reciprocate is guilt-bondage. . . . He who

ELEGANT GESTURES, ELEGANT PORCELAIN

*A delicate hand, elegant spoon, cup, and saucer—the combination of
these elements continued to attract eighteenth-century painters as
subject matter. The culture that sprang up around the hot beverages
differed from that of refined eating, which had also engendered a great
many functional objects and gestures, in that in the former there was
a real need at stake—hunger. Thus dining scenes contrasted with
coffee scenes in the latter's very lack of urgency. Illustrations:*
Breakfast *by Jean de Troy (facing page);* Count and Countess
zu Stolberg-Gedern, *by an anonymous painter (above).*

cannot repay the loan or potlatch loses his rank and even his status as a free man."

Even today traces survive of this original sense of gift giving. Anyone who gives a gift, treats, or invites another is the superior and more powerful person. The recipient, of course, has the advantage of receiving something of value without paying for it; but on the other hand he does pay for it, precisely by being left the passive receiver. For this reason it is mostly children and women—those who in our society personify powerlessness and passivity—who are given gifts. The German expression for reciprocating a gift, *sich revanchieren,* contains a word closely linked to "revenge," a reminder that every gift basically entails an assault on the autonomy of the receiver. This is exactly what Nietzsche, that great unmasker of fair appearances, meant by calling gratitude a form of revenge: expressing thanks when one has received a favor or a present gives an immaterial counterpresent, so to speak, a formula by which the recipient attempts to neutralize or, more accurately, to avenge, the incursion into his existence the gift represents.

Yet these are only lingering traces of the older meaning that gift giving, gift receiving, and the exchange of presents once had. With the capitalist principle of exchange, this mechanism has generally lost its power in our daily lives.

It is only in the context of alcohol drinking that it still survives with any degree of vigor. In a sense, the bar is a thoroughly archaic place, with more than mere vestiges, hints, or sublimations of what once was clinging to it. Here the genuine article lives on: drinkers sharing rounds are participants in a potlatch. With the instinctive sureness of migratory birds they follow the rules and rituals of offering and reciprocating, without an inkling of their ancient origins. Assisting them in this, of course, is the alcohol itself, around which everything revolves. It washes away the newer, "civilized" levels of consciousness, exposing the archaic level where intoxication, fraternity, and competition merge as spontaneously as they might have in a drinking bout five hundred, a thousand, or three thousand years ago.

The modern hot beverages offer nothing comparable to the communal rites of alcohol consumption. Coffee and tea are genuinely bourgeois in this respect too, utterly devoid of the archaic significance of drinking. With coffee and tea there is no clinking of glasses, no toasting, no reciprocal invitation to rounds of drinks. Coffee and tea drinkers form no internally united community; they are only an assemblage of lone individuals. It is altogether normal for patrons of coffeehouses to sit alone at a table, reading a newspaper; the classic games of coffeehouses, billiards and chess, demand concentration on the part of individual players. To put it simply, all rituals in pubs and bars issue from a collectivity, a *we*, while in coffeehouses the *I* is central.

However, just because coffee and tea do not partake of the ritualistic tradition of alcohol does not mean that certain quasi-ritualistic forms have not in turn developed around their consumption.

Coffee- and tea-drinking conventions as we know them today originated in the early eighteenth century. Their history is essentially that of the various utensils developed expressly for these new drinks. The tea or coffee set or service could be considered a reified drinking ritual. Each of its parts—the pot, cup, saucer, spoon, sugar dish, milk pitcher, etc.—requires a specific repertoire of hand gestures, or conversely, in each of these parts a specific canon of gestures has been given concrete expression. The coffee or tea service evinces the same Rococo spirit that made the snuffbox and snuff itself such a highly evolved form of self-expression. In the eighteenth century the coffee- or teacup and the snuffbox were not simply utilitarian objects to be used as efficiently and modestly as possible. A person in the Rococo era used them rather as a pretext for self-display. The manner in which one held a cup, a saucer, a spoon, or brought any of these objects to one's mouth, or set them down, etc., became a social

THE SAUCER'S ORIGINAL FUNCTION

*What is "not done" today was common throughout the eighteenth
century: cooling off coffee by pouring it from the cup into the saucer,
and even drinking out of the saucer. But this, in any case, may have
been strictly a middle-class custom, since illustrations of aristocratic
tea and coffee drinking show saucers used only as a sort of small
salver or tray for the cup (see, e.g., pp. 88 and 90). Because they were
used for drinking, saucers into the nineteenth century were far deeper
and rounder than they are today.*

and cultural mode of identification, no less than one's handling of a snuffbox or one's adroitness in taking a pinch of snuff.

The substances we have been examining have played an essential part in the discovery of the human hand as a vehicle for fashion and self-expression. Each finger of the human hand was assigned specific practical and aesthetic functions. The thumb and index finger were used to take a pinch from the snuffbox and bring it up to one's nose; in another position they held the cup and guided it to the mouth. The little finger was raised, its function purely aesthetic. These are only a few examples of the new gestural code the Rococo created, which has lasted to the present day. It would be fascinating to compile a complete catalogue of the hand and finger positions from eighteenth-century illustrations and to relate them to the new objects which they were designed to hold and manipulate.

From the evolution of the shapes and forms of eighteenth-century drinking utensils, we can deduce which desirable gestures they were designed to accommodate and how some of them even inspired the forms. The cup is a good example. It came from the Orient, together with coffee and tea. The Chinese teacup, like the Arabic coffee cup, had neither a handle nor a saucer. These were European additions. Originally they fulfilled a purely practical function. The handle was to protect the drinker from being burned by the hot drink. The saucer was used to cool off the drink. It was common practice as late as the eighteenth century for even the higher echelons of society to drink out of the saucer, which for that reason was deeper and more convex than it is today. But the original function of handle and saucer was soon abandoned and forgotten, acquiring a purely aesthetic character. Cup and saucer henceforth received more attention as a pair, since they offered greater possibilities for self-display than either cup or bowl did on their own. We still get a small sense of this self-dramatization in the decision over whether to drink the coffee in a cup or in a mug. Coffee in a mug is weekday coffee, coffee in the kitchen—coffee without ceremony. The coffee ritual begins

ENGLISH COFFEEPOT, 1681

The conical form is clearly reminiscent of beer and cider pots, which in the earliest phase of coffee drinking were still used as vessels for the new beverage. (Cf. pp. 54–55, where these pots are clearly recognizable in the background, at the fireplace.)

CHINESE VASE, CONVERTED INTO A COFFEEPOT
*The body of the pot is an imported China vase, to which a metal
spout, handle, and lid of European manufacture had been added.
"Collages" of this sort were by no means rare in the early
eighteenth century.*

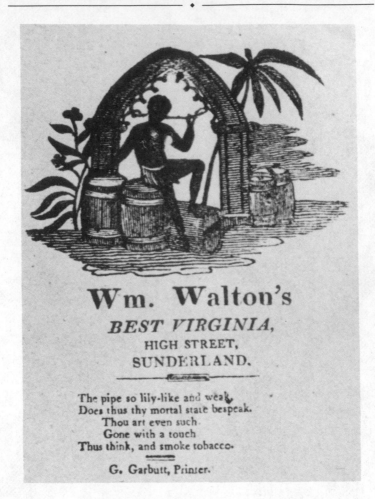

Wm. Walton's

BEST VIRGINIA,

HIGH STREET,

SUNDERLAND.

The pipe so lily-like and weak,
Does thus thy mortal state bespeak.
Thou art even such.
Gone with a touch
Thus think, and smoke tobacco.

G. Garbutt, Printer.

THE EVOLUTION OF TOBACCO ADVERTISING

From the very first, exotic motifs were typical of advertisements for colonial goods. The use of this particular substance, so this message would have it, satisfied fantasies of distant shores. This publicity from a London tobacco dealer already contains the stock images of a palm tree and a "native" (above). Later on, a small story in pictures will be developed from this, including the actual goods acquired amid the palms by the European merchant who then transported them on ships to Europe (facing page). With cigarettes, this reference to the actual "use value" of tobacco was dropped. Women now replaced the exotic (p. 184).

Reiner Ungefärbter.
Amerikanischer Tabak
bei
PH: CAS: KRAFFT & Comp:

only with the saucer, and the more pieces from a service that are brought into play, the more formal it becomes. The enjoyment is due not only to the drink itself, but to the appurtenances that have been created for it.

It is much the same with tobacco-related rituals. As we have seen above, it is not only the pharmacological effect of nicotine that causes the pleasure of smoking. The repertoire of motions and manipulations associated with smoking is equally important. In this respect smoking is closely related to the consumption of hot beverages. The equipment or dishes used in consumption — the pipe, snuffbox, cup—are, as it were, partners in pleasure. The more gestural possibilities the implements permit, the greater the pleasure in manipulating them. We have seen in the evolution of smoking how all these possible variations rapidly dwindled as smoking implements became increasingly simplified. Pipe smoking still requires a whole set of manipulations and accessories. Cigar smoking has eliminated a good many of these. Still, a certain ritualistic character is preserved: cutting the tip, removing the band, forming an ash, etc. Finally this process of simplification, that is, the acceleration of the smoking routine, culminated in the cigarette. The cigarette doesn't require preparatory rituals or manipulations. You simply put it between your lips. Compared to the gestural possibilities that pipes and cigars provided, the cigarette presents a pale, faceless, insipid image. At a time when the traditional forms of smoking were still very much alive, it continually conjured up associations of lightness, ephemerality, unreality—femininity. In 1914 Alexander von Gleichen-Russwurm called it "the child of an age in which charms are fleeting," adding: "It is all promise, never fulfillment, its delicate smoke flies off and only gently, gently does the fine aroma flutter through the room; it has not a trace of obtrusiveness or importunateness about it."

At the turn of the century the cigarette became the symbol of modern life par excellence. It embodied speed, transience, the hectic big city, and advertising. Indeed, it seems to exemplify the principle of modern capitalist production and consumption. Goods are being produced for ever-faster consumption in ever-greater quantities. They lose in "substance or content," but that is replaced by the external "packaging." The actual quality, for instance, the taste of a thing, no longer counts, but rather what would have to be called the illusion or image of the thing is what matters. Things no longer speak for themselves. From now on advertisements define what a thing is. Ads create a world of illusions, within which things are assigned their new place, their new meaning, and the new rituals that surround them. The advertisement for a given product encompasses not only its "promotion," but also "recruitment" and "solicitation"; and in the broad sense the whole culture industry, movies in particular, are part of this advertising and publicity.

As tobacco advertising evolved, we see how it became increasingly detached from the thing or product it represented. In the eighteenth and nineteenth centuries an advertisement was entirely focused on the object: the pictures had to do with tobacco and smoking. Ads for pipe tobacco and cigars were addressed to smokers looking for a specific pleasure in smoking. With cigarette advertising, the item itself had become largely irrelevant. Cigarette ads replaced the older motifs of tobacco and smokers with completely independent pictorial allurements. Cigarettes were no longer promoted for a specific tobacco taste, but with pictures of Monte Carlo and beautiful women. Or if once in a while a specific taste was still being promoted, it was not that of tobacco, but of perfumed tobacco. The thing itself, tobacco, disappeared in the cigarette in two senses: concealed first under the white paper and secondly under added perfumes. Thus the advertising world became embedded in the article itself, penetrating to its very fiber. Gauloises became a brand preferred by smokers who wanted to escape just this sort of imposition (in Marxist terminology this process of the derealization of things is generally known as a disappearance of use value into exchange value).

The disappearance of things through the very publicity created for them would affect the rituals that accompanied their consumption. The cigarette no longer retained a real smoking ritual like those that accompanied pipe and cigar smoking. The traditional ritual had been related to the actual thing—in this case, tobacco. Instead, a new sort of smoking ritual evolved for the cigarette: no longer related to the thing—for that was now masked by advertising—but related to the advertisement. The cigarette smoker's gestures, which constitute the pleasure of smoking, are reenactments of the advertising images. Whether as adjective or noun, "the commercial" pervades our entire culture industry. To hold a cigarette like Greta Garbo, or to screw it into the side of your mouth like Humphrey Bogart—these were the ritualistic smoking gestures for smokers of the 1930s and '40s.

SEVEN

·

Drinking Places

·

*T*hroughout history drinking alcohol has meant creating social bonds. The oldest drinking rites were demonstrations of the fellowship built up among participants. The guest offered a drink of welcome is being symbolically accepted as a part of his host's household. Drinking to someone's health, making toasts, fraternity drinking, drinking in rounds unite participants at least for the duration of their drinking. In no situation is this archaic meaning clearer than in the public drinking place. Here a set of rules and regulations holds sway different from any found outside in normal middle-class life. As an American sociological study puts it: "Public drinking places are 'open regions': those who are present, acquainted or not, have the right to engage others in conversational interaction and the duty to accept the overtures of sociability proffered to them. While many, and perhaps the majority, of conventional settings customarily limit the extent of contact among strangers, sociability is the most general rule in the public drinking place. Although the bar is typically populated primarily by strangers, interaction is available to all those who choose to enter. The physical door through which one enters a drinking establishment is a symbolic door as well, for those who come through it declare by entering that unless they put forth evidence to the contrary, they will be open for conversation with unacquainted others for the duration of their stay. Whatever their age, sex, or apparent position, their biographical blemishes or physical stigmas, all who enter are immediately vested with the status of an open person, open both in having the right to make contact with the others present and in the general obligation of being open to others who may contact them." If this general openness on the part of guests marks the bar or pub as an archaic territory, it remains at the same time a thoroughly modern one, in that the drinks served in it must still be paid for. The barkeeper or publican is not a host, but a merchant. The clientele may for a while suspend the principle of exchange as they embrace and offer one another drinks. But for the barkeeper "host"—apart from any momentary rushes of similar largesse—these "guests" are still customers, served as long as they can still pay.

The conflicting character of the bar, the site of an almost symbolic repeal of the laws of exchange yet at the same time a commercial establishment like any other, can be traced to a long historical process of commercialized hospitality. Before inns, hotels, restaurants, and taverns assumed their present form, various other intermediary forms came and went. Out of the pure hospitality that still prevailed in the early Middle Ages, there arose in the later Middle Ages a transitional form of hospitality in the guest trade run by the corporative estates. The inns for merchants in the great fair- and trading-cities, the so-called merchants' courts, were part of this phenomenon. As for early forms of the tavern, these included urban "drinking rooms," which were also run by the corporative estates and could be called prototypes of

TABLE COMPANIONS IN A DRINKING PARLOR, SIXTEENTH CENTURY
(The Round Table of Jobst Tetzel, *painting from Tetzel's guest book.*)

STUDENT DRINKING AND SMOKING SOCIETY, EIGHTEENTH CENTURY
(A page from the register of the Drinking Fraternity of the Students of Jena.)

MEDIEVAL INN

*Households that sold their surplus of homemade beer or wine
advertised the fact by hanging a bundle of brushwood, a broom, or a
wreath, mounted upon a pole outside their house. Out of this very
primitive form (our illustration dates from the thirteenth century)
there gradually evolved over the centuries the artistic signs that still
hang to this day outside old inns in Germany.*

the later clubs and associations. The city fathers and the individual guilds would meet in these drinking parlors for certain purposes (release of apprentices, funeral feasts, weddings, etc.) as well as when councils were held to discuss the affairs of their own groups and of the city. A drinking code comparable to that of student fraternities prevailed at these meetings.

The public drinking place developed along a quite different line than these associationlike corporative establishments. It was a product of the money economy and of expanded foreign trade, both forces that pulled the rug out from under the older hospitality, replacing it with a "paying-guest trade." Three services were available to the clientele: room, board, and a place to drink. For ages these had existed under one roof; travelers as a rule were offered not only a bed, but also food and drink. Even today this is true of the better hotels, which contain a restaurant and a bar. But for a long time there have also existed special types of establishments to fulfill the separate needs of the guest trade. For eating there was the restaurant (earlier the eating house or "cookshop"), for staying overnight the hotel (earlier the inn), for drinking the pub or bar (earlier the alehouse or tavern). Originally all these sites were barely distinguishable from a private household. Indeed, they started out as private households that simply made whatever surpluses they may have had (of rooms, food, drink) available to strangers, for a price. Only gradually did the guesthouse begin to be commercialized. From the changes in the interior of the public house or tavern, we can see how a once thoroughly private setting gradually was transformed to meet the requirements of a commercial drinking place. This physical transformation took place around the hub of the tavern, the counter.

The Coming of Counters and Bars

Originally the restaurant was identical with the kitchen of the house. The kitchen was more than just the place where food was prepared; it was an all-purpose room. The social life of the restaurant took place around the open hearth—where the food was also prepared—even as late as the eighteenth century. A separate area for guests existed only in the large inns and only for upper-class travelers. The innkeeper's family, the help, and guests mingled in this all-purpose room, or, to put it another way, the guest, for the length of his stay, became part of the innkeeper's family, the only difference being that he paid for the privilege.

The more professionally an inn was run, the larger its "guest room" or restaurant, which no longer functioned as a kitchen. The cooking was relegated to a separate space. The only trace left of it in the restaurant was the open hearth and the (now merely decorative) pots, pans, and crockery on the walls.

Around 1800 the restaurant became separated from the innkeeper's private rooms. It became the commercial space in which the clientele was served. Yet compared to other types of business premises, it still retained an aura of relative privacy, resembling a pleasant parlor that just happened to be open to the public. This was because it was not yet equipped with what had been a permanent feature of the retail trade since the late Middle Ages: a counter marking the concrete boundary across which buyers and sellers dealt with one another. Goods were passed over the counter to enter the possession of the buyer as soon as he laid the required money on it.

The counter first appeared in English restaurants at the beginning of the nineteenth century, and in Anglo-American regions it was known as *the bar*. With this new piece of furniture the restaurant once and for all shed its cozy private character. The bar, like the counter, was never found in private households. Restaurants would now be divided into two areas—the space behind the counter where the innkeeper did his business, and the

The space shown in the drawing Village Inn *(p. 198) and in* Taste *(pp. 196–97) by Adrien von Ostade, is kitchen, guest room, and living room rolled into one for the innkeeper's family. Everything centers on the hearth, the only one in the house. This is still true of the country inn in Rowlandson's early-nineteenth-century drawing (top, p. 199), though here things are already clearly arranged in a new way: the serving staff is now in evidence, as are the guests' places at a table prepared for them. In the background the actual kitchen and the space for the beer tap are already separated by a partition from the area reserved for guests. An urban variant on this transition from kitchen to restaurant is shown in the eighteenth-century illustration of the Parisian establishment Ramponneau (bottom, p. 199). Kitchen and restaurant still form a single spatial unit, but both are already clearly marked off from one another by a divider through which the food and drink customers have ordered is received by the waiters. From the number of tables in the guests' area it is apparent how much business has expanded, thus necessitating this new spatial arrangement. Finally, in both of Cruikshank's illustrations (pp. 200, 201) we see how the "gin palace," a completely new type of drinking place, responded to the increased volume in patronage. The counter, already visible at the Ramponneau, where it still plays a rather minor role, now assumes a central place in the activity, as a sort of traffic island or nodal point at which business is transacted. The restaurant with seating arrangements, if it still exists at all, is separate from the bar, and reached by a small staircase (Parlour Upstairs, p. 200). Customers normally do their drinking standing up at the bar (p. 201). Restaurants were transformed by these conditions only in England and the United States, the bastions of capitalism. In Germany the bar never quite caught on to this degree. Karl Kautsky had the Gemütlichkeit of German taverns in mind when he wrote of English bars in 1891: "The English tavern is merely a shop in which spirits are sold; it is set up so that no one could possibly feel tempted to linger longer than necessary to empty a glass, which one does, in fact, while standing at the service counter. In such a place there is not a trace of camaraderie or exchange of ideas."*

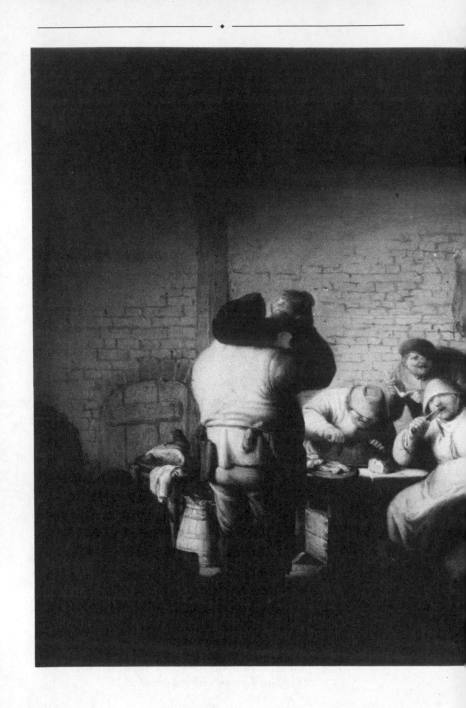

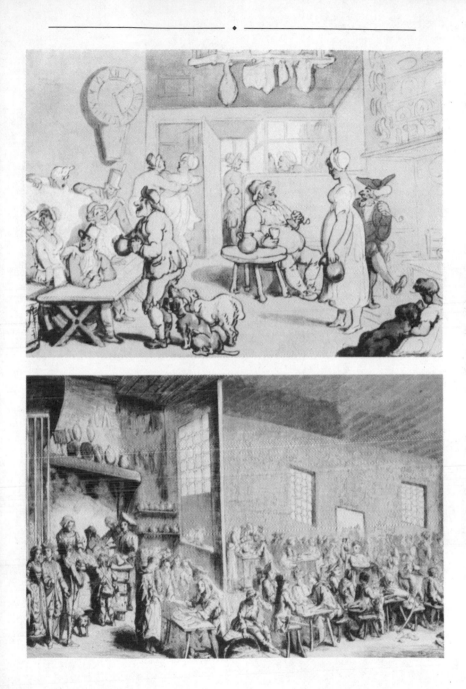

actual restaurant. But the counter-turned-bar soon took on another significance besides the purely commercial one. Standing at this bar became the typical way of having a drink in such an establishment, which itself eventually became known as a "bar." The reason for this was the physical proximity of the tavern-keeper and the fact that the bar was not only a counter but the location of the taps for drinks. Physical proximity to the bar clearly stirred atavistic memories of the tavernkeeper's original role as host—in total contrast to the commercial significance of the bar as a counter, that is, a counting place where money changed hands.

The fact that the bar first made its way into the big-city drinking houses of England, the so-called gin places, at the start of the nineteenth century marks it as a genuine product of the Industrial Revolution. In this respect it could be compared to distilled spirits, or be termed their architectural equivalent. If because of its high alcohol content liquor sped up the inebriation process, the bar sped up, i.e., shortened, the length of a drinker's stay in the bar. Liquor is not consumed slowly in long sips, but abruptly "tossed off." The process is so quick that it can be performed standing up. Because of their bars, the gin places that were springing up like mushrooms in Manchester and other English industrial cities at the start of the nineteenth century resembled factory assembly lines. One such establishment in Manchester served over 400 customers in an hour. In a single week the fourteen largest gin palaces in London served 270,000 guests—almost a metropolis unto itself. Thus it seems no exaggeration to characterize the bar as a *traffic* innovation, or as the historians Gorham and Dunnett have written, "a solution to a traffic problem just as much as Haussmann's Place de l'Etoile or a Woolworth store are practical solutions." The bar introduced a qualitative innovation to the traffic flow of the gin palace. It sped up drinking, just as the railroad sped up travel and the mechanical loom sped up textile production.

However, only in England and the United States did bars and

saloons change so thoroughly. Since the nineteenth century the Anglo-American drinking saloon has been called simply a "bar": bar and public drinking space had merged.

On the Continent and particularly in Germany the bar, that is, the actual bar behind which the bartender stands, never acquired this exact significance. Compared to the long American bar, the German bar-counter is a mere stump. The French bar is halfway between these two extremes—the lesson being that one of the ways to gauge the extent to which commercialism has saturated a given culture is by the length of its bars. The bar functioned mainly as a place from which to serve drinks, rinse glasses, etc. While drinking at a bar is normal in England and the United States, in Germany it has become the unspoken prerogative of regulars only. To this day people in German *Kneipen* (taverns) drink at tables. The prevailing atmosphere is one which even the English language calls *Gemütlichkeit*.

EIGHT

·

The Artificial Paradises of the Nineteenth Century

·

> If I weren't afraid of hashish, I'd stuff
> myself with it as though it were bread.
> —Flaubert

Every society has the pleasure goods, stimulants, and inebriants it deserves, needs, and can tolerate. Since classical antiquity the chief intoxicant of western civilization has been alcohol. In whatever forms it has been consumed—as wine, beer, or hard liquor—it has become so permanent an element of our culture, we cannot imagine life without it. There have always been attempts to do away with alcohol. But these have only been quixotic episodes, as American Prohibition of the 1920s has shown most recently. Yet the temperance movements have very convincing arguments at their disposal. The socially destructive consequences of alcoholism are all too obvious. Alcohol addiction is one of the most devastating ills of our civilization. That its material cause, alcohol, should be so firmly anchored in our culture demonstrates an apparent need for it.

The same cannot be said of the group of narcotics that have achieved such a tremendous significance in other cultures but never really gained a foothold in Europe. These drugs might be referred to as intoxicants—and "poison" translates the *toxin* in intoxicant quite literally—a designation the bitterest ideological opponents of alcohol have applied to it too. Rudolf Gelpke, a cultural critic in the tradition of Nietzsche and Ernst Jünger, points out that these toxic substances, or poisons, "are not just this or that substance; rather they are specific substances that, in specific *dosages,* produce a 'toxic' effect on a specific organism. Thus the same substance in different dosages can be used either as a narcotic or as a poison. . . . There is only one possibility for an objective justification of the term 'intoxicant' applied to drugs, and that is the equation of *intoxication* and *poisoning.* Anyone who reasons and judges in this way, at least is doing so precisely and rigorously. But in that case he must be consistent, and without exception judge *every* instance of inebriation as a 'case of poisoning.' Furthermore, he must pretty much put *alcohol* at the top of his blacklist of 'intoxicants' or poisons. . . . Apart from members of certain sects, Europeans would more or less instinctively find it ridiculous to speak of wine as a 'narcotic.' And rightly so: it *is* ridiculous. But these same Europeans would also consider it entirely valid if in keeping with the technological Westernization of the planet, and with the help of various organizations and commissions . . . Asians, Indians, and other non-Caucasians were to be forbidden *their* 'narcotics' by an appeal to an ostensibly objective science that designated them as 'intoxicants,' poisons."

The taboo on narcotics (opium, hashish, marijuana, cocaine, heroin, morphine, etc.) and their being made illegal in today's world happened fairly recently. Until the end of the nineteenth century narcotics were treated and used in a laissez-faire manner. How freely and naively they were used, and with what consequences, is exemplified in the history of opium.

Opium, the Proletariat, and Poetry

At the beginning of the nineteenth century opium was commonly available as a sedative and painkiller. It was used somewhat as aspirin is today and had a regular place in the family medicine chest. The family doctor prescribed it like any other medication. It was freely obtainable in pharmacies at a relatively reasonable price and was taken to overcome hysterical and nervous conditions, motion sickness, migraines, etc. Perhaps its most significant use was in juices and syrups given to children to lull them to sleep. The prominent opium addicts of the century usually traced the start of their addiction to just such dosing with opiates in childhood.

In any case, not only did opium have an assured place in the middle-class medicine chest, it was also an integral part of the lives of the working class. Marx, who coined the phrase that religion was "the opiate of the people," knew very well that the people of his day actually consumed opium: "Just as it is in the English factory districts, so too in the agricultural districts opium consumption is expanding day by day among adult workers, male and female." The retail sale and consumption of opium became considerable, almost comparable to the volume of business in taverns. According to one report from this period, "in every village in the surrounding area there was a store in which laudanum bottles [laudanum being a solution of alcohol and opium, the commonest form of opium consumption] were stored by the hundreds, ready for purchase by the workers as they streamed out of their factories on Saturdays." Thomas De Quincey, in his *Confessions of an English Opium-Eater,* has left us a vivid depiction of the casualness, ease, and cheapness with which opium was made available to the working population: "These respectable London druggists, in widely remote quarters of London, from whom I happened lately to be purchasing small quantities of opium, assured me that the number of *amateur* opium-eaters (as I may term them) was, at this time, immense; . . . This evidence respected London only. But (and this will possibly surprise the reader more) some years ago, on passing through Manchester, I was informed by several cotton manufacturers that their work-people were rapidly getting into the practice of opium-eating; so much so, that on a Saturday afternoon the counters of the druggists were strewed with pills of one, two, or three grains, in preparation for the known demand of the evening. The immediate occasion of this practice was the lowness of wages, which, at that time, would not allow them to indulge in ale or spirits; and, wages rising, it may be thought that this practice would cease."

This ordinary acceptance of opium by the working-class population in the first half of the nineteenth century has been somewhat overshadowed by the generally better-known fact that the artistic and literary avant-garde of the same period consumed opium extensively, as well as hashish (drugs which at this time were closely interrelated). De Quincey, Coleridge, Poe, Baudelaire, Nerval, Théophile Gautier, to name only the most famous writers, were notorious users of opium and hashish. The Paris "Club des Hachischins" equated literary production with drug consumption and made it part of their agenda. The opium and hashish generation of the nineteenth century were Romantics. They proclaimed the artist an asocial figure. Life and work were to become one, to be radically set apart from a bourgeois world that was increasingly viewed as objectionable. Instead, artists and aesthetes escaped to an ersatz land of fantasy, the Orient. Opium and hashish, drugs from the Orient, transplanted poetic fantasy (in an almost physiological sense) into this landscape. The journey into the fantasy-Orient that the opium poet embarked upon in his dream became a work of art in his subsequent writings. Life and art thus became one, and both were dreamlike, unreal, asocial. Baudelaire explicitly formulated his preference for hashish over wine as part of a program of asociality. For him, alcoholic intoxication was fundamentally a predictable, controllable, rational, bourgeois affair; whereas hashish smoking was *evil* in the sense of his famous poetry collection *The Flowers of Evil*—that

OPIUM DEN IN LONDON'S EAST END, CA. 1870
(Woodcut by Gustave Doré.)

WOMEN WORKERS SMOKING OPIUM IN NEW YORK, END OF THE
NINETEENTH CENTURY

is, asocial, egocentric, destructive: "Wine heightens the will, hashish abolishes it. Wine sustains the body, hashish is a suicide weapon. Wine makes one good and peaceable. Hashish isolates. . . . Why, in truth, should one work, toil, write, create, or what have you, if in a sudden moment one can attain paradise? In short, wine is for people who work and who thus win the right to drink it. But hashish belongs to the solitary joys; it was created for hapless idlers." This view of the effects of hashish is one which today every police chief might agree with; only the conclusions he would draw from it would be the opposite of Baudelaire's.

In actual practice the nineteenth-century opium and hashish poets performed a remarkable, quite unintended function. The sheer vividness of their formulations gave middle-class society ample ammunition with which to outlaw these drugs. It took the poetic imagination and antibourgeois feelings of the poets in describing opium and hashish as means for the expansion and dissolution of the self to shock society out of its indifference. The publication of these dream-poems first made society aware of these previously hidden effects of the drugs. It was the asocial significance attributed by the poets to opium and hashish which first caused them to lose their identity as ordinary household remedies. Suddenly they emerge as dangerous narcotics, and as such, threats to the bourgeois individual. Of course, that does not mean modern drug legislation would not have come about eventually even without the opium literature of the nineteenth century. It would be absurd to advance such a simplistic view of cause and effect. In the course of the nineteenth century the *real* dangers of narcotics were amply revealed. Nevertheless, the control measures and prohibitions with which society tried to protect itself were another matter altogether. The emotional atmosphere in which these measures were implemented was a realm unto itself. The deep-seated fear of any contact with these drugs, which at least until a few years ago still characterized the attitude toward narcotics, cannot be fully explained by the actual dangers. Bour-

OPIUM DREAMS

*John Martin, who, unlike his literary contemporaries Thomas De
Quincey and Coleridge, was not an "opium-eater," nonetheless gave
permanent form in his fantastic visions to the dreams that others
experienced in states of intoxication. Pictures like* Belshazzar's Feast
from 1826 (pp. 212–13) or The Fall of Nineveh *of 1829 (above) reveal
a fascination with the same blend of orgiastic and destructive power
that enraptured and tormented the "opium-dreamers." De Quincey
wrote of opium in 1822: "Thou buildest upon the bosom of darkness,
out of the fantastic imagery of the brain, cities and temples, beyond
the art of Phidias and Praxiteles—beyond the splendor of Babylon and
Hekatompylos; and, 'from the anarchy of dreaming sleep,' callest into
sunny light the faces of long-buried beauties and the blessed
household countenances, cleansed from the 'dishonors of the grave.' "
The enthusiasm for all things oriental that swept Europe in this period
reached its absolute peak with the opium dreams of the poets and the
images of John Martin.*

geois anxiety fantasies were the mirror images of the poets' dreams—not quite so poetic, of course, yet unmistakably their reflections.

Other discoveries also contributed to the fact that by the end of the nineteenth century narcotics were no longer regarded or used as naively as they had been in the first half of the century. First among these was the recognition of the phenomenon of addiction, of the actual forming of a habit. Thomas de Quincey's *Confessions of an English Opium-Eater* was written as the case history of an addict fully aware of his addiction. The production of morphine (1817) and heroin (1874) from opium had the same effect on the drug scene as the spread of hard liquor had had on the drinking world: an escalation of toxicity with considerable consequences for society. Morphine in particular added a new dimension to the drug problem. It was used in massive quantities for the first time in military hospitals during the great wars of the nineteenth century—the Crimean War, the American Civil War—then in the First World War. The wars multiplied the incidence of drug addiction. Morphine made its way from military into civilian life, a process of expansion we have already observed for tobacco in and after the Thirty Years' War.

Because of these pharmacological and sociological developments drug addiction now became a social phenomenon that could no longer be ignored. Yet the legislators of the liberal laissez-faire state balked at taking drastic measures. One of the earliest drug-control laws, the English "Pharmacy and Poisons Act" of 1868, decreed what was already customary procedure: that opium was to be sold only in pharmacies; and that how much and to whom it was sold remained at the discretion of the pharmacist. (Poisons were treated just as liberally. Here the law stated only that the pharmacist had to know the customer personally.)

The decisive impetus for modern drug legislation eventually came from outside Europe. It was the fateful role opium had played in China. The Chinese opium question sparked one of the great moral and political campaigns of the nineteenth century, comparable in its fervor only to the opposition to slavery. The antiopium campaign culminated in a series of international treaties negotiated shortly before and after the First World War, with the goal of curbing the international opium trade. Only in the wake of these agreements did the individual countries promulgate national drug laws, which in essence remain in effect to the present day.

Opium and Colonialism

From the nineteenth century to the present day, western public opinion has seen Chinese culture as an opium culture. Yet it had become that only two or three centuries earlier. Up until the eighteenth century opium had been used in China as much, that is to say as little, as in Europe. The Chinese made its closer acquaintance only with European "help," largely that of the English East India Company. The company had enjoyed a lively trade relationship with the Chinese Empire ever since the seventeenth century. The various chinoiseries that were all the rage among the European upper classes—tea, silk, porcelain—represented lucrative items of trade. In the seventeenth and early eighteenth centuries, when the Middle Empire was still an equal partner of the European powers, these articles were regularly paid for in cash, because the Chinese had no use for anything the Europeans could offer them in exchange.

However, the situation changed during the eighteenth century when the Chinese Empire grew proportionately weaker as the European powers, above all England, became more and more aggressive. Trade between equal partners was transformed into a trade dictatorship by the East India Company, which enforced its will by means of its own militia. Instead of continuing to pay for Chinese products in cash, the company now offered a special trade item, opium. It was a cheap commodity for the company, produced on a large scale on its plantations in India. Estimates are

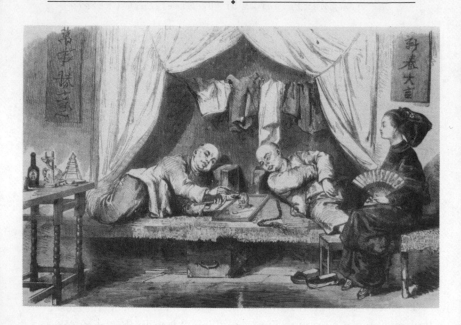

OPIUM SMOKING IN CHINA

Opium smoking became a regular part of daily life at the end of the eighteenth century. Although opium was repeatedly prohibited, all levels of society used it, much in the way Europeans smoked tobacco. The smoking took place at home, when entertaining a business friend (facing page), or in establishments that were open to the public in the same way as inns and coffeehouses (above).

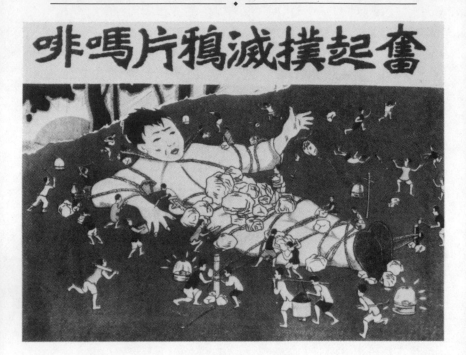

OPIUM AND IMPERIALISM

*This 1911 poster depicts China's predicament from the Nationalists'
viewpoint: the Chinese giant, in chains and held down by the boulders
of the opium addiction that had been forced on it by foreign powers.*

that between 1767 and 1850, in less than a century, Chinese opium consumption increased seventyfold. Obviously such an increase brought far-reaching social consequences. The comparison with the English gin epidemic immediately springs to mind. One might also compare the role opium played in China since the eighteenth century with that of coffee in Europe since the seventeenth century: the stagnation of sociopolitical life in China, one might say, was reflected in opium consumption, just as the early capitalist activity of western Europe was reflected in its coffee consumption.

The spread of opium through Chinese society cut across all classes of the population, from very low to very high. The report of a western missionary from 1868 contains this description of the situation: "Large Chinese commercial firms keep opium on hand for their business friends. On house calls the best physicians expect to be invited to a pipe of opium and resent it if such an invitation is not forthcoming. Administrative officials and the police are prepared for a policy, urgent as it may be, when they have first smoked a pipe of opium. In well-to-do families the accessories necessary to opium smoking are a regular feature of the household. . . . The vice of opium smoking has for a long time threatened the welfare and the prosperity of this people. In all parts of the Empire the consumption of opium is rapidly rising. Its calamitous consequences grow increasingly evident. More and more frequently one sees the unfortunate victims, and in ever larger numbers. The establishments it is offered in grow more numerous, and the nation grows increasingly poor."

The socially destructive consequences of opium use were first revealed in the late eighteenth century; in the early nineteenth century they had begun to assume catastrophic proportions. The Chinese government tried repeatedly to resist the compulsory trade by prohibiting opium smoking—but to no avail. In the notorious opium wars resistance was finally crushed by military force, and opium legalized: a classic instance of colonial gunboat diplomacy.

THE OPIUM INDUSTRY OF THE EAST INDIA COMPANY
*The drug that was poured into China was produced on a vast scale.
After the opium pulp had been boiled, it was placed in smaller
containers and set out to dry in a huge storage chamber (above), then
stored for eventual shipping in enormous warehouses (facing page).*

"It is no accident," one commentary on this chapter in colonial history runs, "that the decisive dates in the history of the opium problem fall within the same time span as the loss of self-determination of East Asian peoples" (Wissler). For European colonialism the opium trade was a means of killing two birds with one stone: opium yielded huge profits, and it rendered its buyers docile. Someone dreaming opium dreams is not going to formulate anticolonial thoughts, much less act.

It is astounding how deliberately and systematically the colonial masters were able to deploy opium to this end. They took it for granted, of course, that this commodity was to be used only outside their homeland. Warren Hastings, the governor general of Bengal, declared that opium, not being a necessity of life but a "pernicious" article of luxury, ought not to be permitted, except for purposes of foreign commerce, and took the position that the government should stop its internal consumption. The East India Company itself, the instigator and chief beneficiary of the opium trade, declared in a statement of 1813 how repugnant a thing it considered opium. Insisting it wasn't the company's desire to stimulate demand for opium in England, the statement proposed raising the price of the drug in Britain and its overseas possessions to the highest possible levels, adding that if it were possible to stop its use entirely, except for medicinal purposes, the company would be ready to do its part in the interest of mankind.

However naively and unrestrainedly opium was consumed in nineteenth-century Europe, comparison with opium-drugged semicolonial China shows that an unconscious—one might say instinctual—control was nonetheless being imposed on it. That several dozen Romantic poets abandoned themselves to opium, and that even thousands of workers used it as a substitute for alcohol, hardly matters. Compared with what was going on in China, opium in Europe remained a peripheral drug.

The sound instinct with which the West kept opium out of its own system is demonstrated by the balance sheet of the English East India Company. The handsome profits this corporation made with its sale of opium to the Chinese was only one side of the ledger. The other side was the importation of Chinese tea to England. Tea, the beverage that was to keep English society fit to carry out its great global undertakings, was paid for with opium, which made Chinese society indolent, dreamy, inactive, uncompetitive—manageable. "Put in its simplest form, England sold China opium in exchange for tea, mainly through the agency of the East India Company. . . . in 1831, for example, China bought £11 million worth of opium from the 'country firms' of India, which let the East India Company have £8 million (against bills drawn on London) to spend on tea" (Teff). Opium for tea—a formula which not only explains the successes of English imperialism in the Far East, but which thoroughly typified Europe's relationship to the Third World.

The New Tolerance

Regular drug use is habit-forming. Even though at first the effect is powerfully exciting or intoxicating, it levels off with habitual use. This is true not only for individuals, but also for entire cultures. Every historically significant shift in a cultural pattern of consumption is in essence nothing other than the habituation of large masses of people to once-new stimulants and inebriants. "Perhaps," as Ernst Jünger remarked about wine, "over millennia of use its original power became tamed. We find something far more powerful, but also more sinister, in those myths in which Dionysus, with his train of satyrs, sileni, maenads, and beasts, appears as the lord of the feast." All the exotic spices, stimulants, and intoxicants introduced to European civilization in modern times have gone through this process, becoming habitual or domesticated. The fantastic expectations and fears with which seventeenth-century Europeans greeted coffee, tobacco, and the other exotic substances are gone today, as much as the spirit of

Dionysus from a modern middle-class wine party. The stimulants which by their very novelty once shook mankind to the core have become ordinary everyday rites.

Only the narcotics, like opium, hashish, marijuana, etc., have not yet been included in this breaking-in process to become routine. For that reason they have remained outside of the mass consumption that alone stamps a culture. In this respect they may be compared with the early middle-class stimulants in the seventeenth century. Three hundred years ago coffee, tobacco, etc., were still controversial substances, often officially prohibited, in any case anything but established commodities. Only in the course of the eighteenth century did they win acceptance. Demand for them proved too strong and too constant to be suppressed. Society and the state acted accordingly, and instead of prohibitions, taxes were levied on these new semiluxuries. Under Frederick II, the tobacco tax alone accounted for an eleventh of the revenues of the Prussian state.

There are indications that a very similar development might take place with today's illegal narcotics (which, as we have seen, first became illegal only a short time ago). For some time now, and despite all attempts to reverse the trend, there has been a perceptible relaxation of the prevailing attitude toward them. Until about 1960, this attitude among the western nations had been marked by a sort of fear of contact. These drugs were seen as substances that altered the conscious mind or worse still, dissolved personal identity and thus endangered the very fabric of bourgeois society. This consensus has crumbled since the 1960s. A new attitude emerged among the trend-setting, ideologically influential sectors of the population more or less simultaneously with the liberalization of sexuality. The fear of contact gave way to a new curiosity. Traditional opinions about the effects of drugs were questioned. Drugs were regarded as the possible keys to a new sensibility. In the youth culture of the 1960s popular catchwords such as "expansion of the personality," "consciousness-raising," "self-realization," etc., were intimately related to drug

use. The generation that smoked hashish and marijuana disso-
ciated itself symbolically and pharmacologically from the alcohol-
drinking generation that preceded them, just as that generation
conversely felt menaced by the drug consumption of the younger
generation. The "joint" became a symbol of this youth movement. Cigarette smoking and alcohol drinking stood for achieve-
ment, authority, and so on, hashish and marijuana for liberation
from all such values.

This interpretation, a typical product of the 1960s, is in the
process of disappearing together with the last offshoots of the
youth movement. Yet drug use itself is evidently more than a
passing fad. In the most advanced western industrial nation, the
United States, marijuana smoking has become so widespread that
the existing laws against it appear increasingly nominal. Efforts
are under way in several states (California and New York, for
example) to adapt legislation to the new reality—in other words,
to legalize drugs. It seems plausible, almost foreseeable, that
hashish and marijuana will someday join the ranks of common
pleasure goods as tobacco did three hundred years ago, for the
simple reason that its prohibition creates greater social problems
than its—controlled—legalization

In the United States, in the course of discussions of these issues, drugs have come to be separated into two categories. People
now refer to them as either *soft* or *hard*. Hashish and marijuana
are among the former, heroin and LSD the latter. The meaning
of the distinction is obvious. It involves reaching some prelimi-
nary decision as to whether these drugs are socially acceptable.
Defining the popular drugs hashish and marijuana as soft, that is,
as fundamentally harmless, can be seen as a first step toward their
legalization. By the same token, the designation of LSD, heroin,
etc., as hard drugs means that society and the state have drawn
the line here, and stepping over it remains subject to punishment.
"Marijuana is less toxic than tobacco and milder than liquor"—
with this rather slipshod formulation the late Margaret Mead
summed up the newly prevalent opinion about soft drugs. In

other words, when hashish and marijuana were declared soft drugs, they were removed from the sinister world of narcotics and placed instead in "harmless" proximity to tobacco and alcohol, a crucial step on the way of their transformation from "dangerous narcotics" to "pleasure goods."

More or less at the same time that this new view of drugs was developing, the attitude toward tobacco was changing, in the opposite direction, in fact. While drug use has been expanding, smoking has been on the wane. Numerous scientific investigations have proven the hazardous effects of smoking. Nowhere has this led to an outright prohibition, but there are clear signs that it has led to a curtailment of smoking. Once again it is the United States that has gone furthest in this direction. Smoking is forbidden in an increasing number of public places. For years cigarette companies have been bound by law to add to their advertisements the warning that "cigarette smoking may be harmful to your health." The social and cultural stigmatization of smoking has been most effective in the same sectors of the population that, in their quest for alternative lifestyles, also discovered soft drugs. The decline in smoking and the increased use of soft drugs are closely related and lead to certain conclusions. These circumstances might herald a major shift in pleasure consumption similar to that in which coffee and tobacco were first introduced three hundred years ago. Should soft drugs one day become commonly available for mass consumption in a "postindustrial" society (for want of a better term), this would define the new quality of this society much as coffee and tea consumption defined the then-new society three hundred years ago. The analogy can be taken even further. Just as seventeenth-century prohibitions against coffee and tobacco were desperate rearguard actions on the part of a medieval worldview (which rightly sniffed out the modern, bourgeois dynamic inherent in the new pleasure goods), today's still-enforced prohibition of drugs may be interpreted as a last-ditch effort to maintain the rationality and self-discipline of middle-class life.

AFTERWORD TO THE
AMERICAN EDITION

The preceding sentences about a new tolerance, written in 1979, sound hopelessly out of date in 1992. We all know that the eighties saw a fundamental change in the way we look upon drugs. The decade returned to a traditional intolerance, as David F. Musto, the historian of medicine, noted in 1987 in his new edition of *The American Disease: Origins of Narcotic Control*, a book first published in 1973. Far from having replaced tobacco, both hashish and marijuana have come to share the same social stigma. But of course this too will not be the last word in society's dialogue with drugs. America's history of drug use during the nineteenth and twentieth centuries, Musto demonstrates, is a history of more or less regular fluctuations between periods of tolerance and intolerance. One might add that they are not mechanical swings like those of a pendulum. Each time changes in the taste for drugs occur, they are peculiar to their respective historical period.

At first glance, it would seem that the new intolerance of the eighties failed to produce a substitute drug to make up for the lost pleasures of the tolerance it replaced. In fact, however, what came to assume a dominating role in the culture of taste and pleasure during those years was a substance viewed more like the opposite of pleasure and taste until then. Water, a very basic substance with a totally neutral taste, came to be celebrated as the height of gustatory delight. The European mineral waters Perrier and Pellegrino achieved a status approaching that of Moët-Chandon and Mumm. No doubt there is some truth in the usual explanation for this phenomenon—that it is a fashionable celebration of a healthy and natural lifestyle. But it fails to take into account that for the yuppies of the eighties, mineral water actually *was* a gustatory delight. If we assume that every drug stimulates the narcissistic nature of the individual—his self-pleasure—then the fad for mineral waters in the eighties may well have been a unique chapter in the history of drugs; totally neutral in itself, indeed the very neutrality of water, now venerated as a chic drink of prestige, transported its consumer to a yet-unknown level of narcissistic well-being.

W. S.

BIBLIOGRAPHY

General Works

Bibra, Ernst von, *Die narkotischen Genussmittel und der Mensch*, Nürnberg, 1855.

Blum, Richard H., *Society and Drugs*, San Francisco, 1970.

————, *Students and Drugs*, San Francisco, 1969.

Brillat-Savarin, Anthelme, *Physiologie du goût.*

Hartwich, C., *Die menschlichen Genussmittel: Ihre Herkunft, Verbrei tung, Geschichte, Anwendung, Bestandteile und Wirkung*, Leipzig, 1911.

Hémardinquer, Jean-Jacques, ed., *Pour une historie de l'alimentation*, Paris, 1970 (collected essays from the journal *Annales*).

Kant, Immanuel, *Anthropologie, Erster Teil, Erstes Buch, par. 29.*

Krünitz, Johann Georg, Oeconomische Encyclopädie, Brünn, 1787ff. (entries: *Bier, Branntwein, Caffee, Chocolate, Thee, Taback*, etc.)

Lewin, Louis, *Phantastika: Die betäubenden und erregenden Genuss-mittel*, Berlin, 1927.

Moleschott, Jacob, *Der Kreislauf des Lebens*, Mainz, 1852.

————, *Die Physiologie der Nahrungsmittel*, Darmstadt, 1850.

Reich, Eduard, *Die Nahrungs- und Genussmittelkunde*, Göttingen, 1860 (2 vols.).

Tannahill, Reay, *Food in History*, New York, 1973.

Teuteberg, Hans J., and Wiegelmann, Günter, *Der Wandel der Nah-rungsgewohnheiten unter dem Einfluss der Industrialisierung*, Göttingen, 1972.

Tiedemann, Friedrich, *Physiologie des Menschen*, Darmstadt, 1836 (in particular vol. 3, par. 221).

SPICES IN THE MIDDLE AGES

Austin, Thomas, ed., *Two Fifteenth-century Cookery Books (Harleian MSS. 279 and 4016)*, London 1888 (Early English Text Society, Original Series, no. 91).

Cosman, Madeleine Pelner, *Fabulous Feasts: Medieval Cookery and Ceremony*, New York, 1976.

Dickenmann, J. J., *Das Nahrungswesen in England vom 12. bis 15. Jahrhundert* (in *Anglia*, Jg. xxvii, pp. 453–515).

Furnivall, F. J., *Early English Meals and Manners*, London, 1868 (Early English Text Society, Original Series, no. 32).

Grupp, George, *Kulturgeschichte des Mittelalters*, Stuttgart, 1894.

Henisch, Bridget Ann. *Feast and Fast*, University Park and London, 1976.

Heyd, W., *Geschichte des Levantehandels im Mittelalter*, Stuttgart, 1879 (2 vols.).

Heyne, Moritz, *Das deutsche Nahrungswesen, von den ältesten ge-schichtlichen Zeiten bis zum 16. Jahrhundert*, Leipzig, 1901.

Mead, W. E., *The English Medieval Feast*, London, 1931 (2nd ed., 1967).

Parry, John W., *Spices*, New York, 1969.

Pirenne, Henri, *Economic and Social History of Medieval Europe*, London, 1936.

Schulte, Alwin, *Deutsches Leben im 14. und 15. Jahrhundert*, Vienna, 1892.

Warburg, Otto, *Die Muskatnuss: Geschichte, Botanik, Kultur*, 1897.

Webb, Margaret J., *Early English Recipes, Selected from the Harleian MS. 279 of about 1430*, Cambridge, 1837.

Coffee, Tea, Chocolate

Blegni, Nicolas de, *Le Bon Usage du Thé, du Café et du Chocolat*, Lyon, 1687.

Born, Max von, *Rokoko: Frankreich im 18. Jahrhundert*, Berlin, 1923.

Bradley, Richard, *The Virtue and Use of Coffee, with Regard to the Plague, and other Infectious Distempers*, London, 1721.

Bramah, Edward, *Tea and Coffee*, London, 1972.

Cadet-de-Vaux, Antoine Alexis, *Dissertation sur le Café*, Paris, 1807.

Cheney, Ralph Holt, *Coffee: A Monograph of the Economic Species of the Genus Coffea*, New York, 1925.

Delrue-Schrevens, L., *Le café: Etude historique et commerciale*, Tournais, 1886.

Dufour, Philippe Sylvestre, *Traitez Nouveau et curieux du café, du thé et du chocolate*, Lyon, 1685.

Ellis, Aytoun, *The Penny Universities: A History of the Coffee Houses*, London, 1956.

Fincke, Heinrich, *Handbuch der Kakaoerzeugung*, Berlin, 1936 (includes a historical section).

Forrest, Dennys, *Tea for the British: The Social and Economic History of a Famous Trade*, London, 1973.

Fosca, F., *Histoire des cafés de Paris*, Paris, 1934.

Franklin, Alfred, *Le café, le thé et le chocolat*, Paris, 1893 (vol. 13 in the series "la vie privée d'autrefois").

Gibb, D. E. W., *Lloyd's of London: A Study in Individualism*, London, 1957.

Gleichen-Russwurm, Alexander von, *Das galante Europa*, 1911.

Goubard d'Aulnay, G.-E., *Monographie du café*, Paris, 1832.

Hahnemann, Samuel, *Der Kaffee in seinen Wirkungen*, Leipzig, 1803.

Heinrich, Eduard Jacob, *Sage und Siegeszug des Kaffees*, Hamburg, 1952 (2nd ed.)

Hewitt, Robert, *Coffee: Its History, Cultivation and Uses*, New York, 1872.

Hoffmann, Paul, "Aus dem ersten Jahrhundert des Kaffees" (in *Archiv für Kulturgeschichte*, vol. 8, pp. 405–41; vol. 9, pp. 90–104).

Jünger, Wolfgang, *Herr Ober, ein' Kaffee*, Munich, 1955.

Krüger, Johann Gottlob, *Gedancken vom Caffee, Thee und Toback*. Halle, 1743.

Leussink, Gernhard Arie Günter, *Der Einfluss des Tee-, Kaffee- und Tabakgenusses auf die menschliche Gesundheit im Urteil deutscher Wochenzeitschriften, Zeitungen und Intelligenzblätter im Zeitraum von etwa 1730 bis 1780* (typed dissertation, Münster, 1957).

Lillywhite, Bryan, *London Coffee Houses: A Reference Book*, London, 1963.

Linné, Carl von. *Gedanken vom Kaffee* (in *Nützliche Sammlungen*, 86. Stück, Hannover, 1758). (The article was published anonymously, but is listed in Wolf Müller's bibliography of Linné.)

Lippmann, Edmund O. von, *Geschichte des Zuckers*, Berlin, 1929 (2nd ed.).

Michelet, Jules, *La Régence (Histoire de France*, vol. 15), Paris, 1863.

Moseley, Benjamin, *Abhandlung von den Eigenschaften und Wirkungen des Kaffee*, Lübeck, 1886 (2nd German ed. of the English original).

Müller, Wolf, *Bibliographie des Kaffees, des Kakao, der Schokolade, des Tee und deren Surrogate*, Bad Bocklet, 1960. (Bibliotheca Bibliographica.)

―――, *Seltsame Frucht Kakao*, Hamburg, 1957.

Robinson, Edward, *The Early English Coffee House*, London, 1893 (reprint 1973).

Roque, Jean de la, *Voyage de l'Arabie Heureuse*, Amsterdam, 1716.

Rothfos, Bernard, ed., *Coffea Curiosa*, Hamburg, 1968.

Routh, Harold, "Steele and Addison" (in *The Cambridge History of English Literature*).

Rumford, Benjamin, Count of, *Of the excellent qualities of coffee, and the art of making it . . .* London, n.d. (ca. 1800).

Savary des Bruslons, Jacques, *Dictionnaire universal de commerce,* Paris, 1723 (entries: Café, thé, chocolat).

Schiedlausky, Günther, *Tee, Kaffee, Schokolade: Ihr Eintritt in die europäische Gesellschaft,* Munich, 1961.

Schöner, Erich, *Das Viererschema in der antiken Humoralpathologie* (in *Sudhoffs Archiv,* Beiheft 4, 1964).

Schwarzkopf, S. A., *Der Kaffee in naturhistorischer, diätetischer und medizinischer Hinsicht,* Weimar, 1881.

Tornius, Valerian, *Das Buch über die Schokolade,* Leipzig, 1931.

Toth, Karl, *Weib und Rokoko in Frankreich.*

Ukers, William H., *All About Coffee,* New York, 1922.

———, *All About Tea,* New York, 1935.

Welter, Henri, *Essai sur l'histoire du café,* Paris, 1868.

Westerfrölke, Hermann, *Englische Kaffeehäuser als Sammelpunkte der literarischen Welt im Zeitalter von Dryden und Addison,* Jena, 1924.

ALCOHOLIC BEVERAGES, DRINKING RITUALS AND PLACES

Adler, Viktor, *Gesammelte Reden und Schriften zur Alkoholfrage,* Vienna, 1922.

Bauer, Max. *Der deutsche Durst: Methyologische Skizzen aus der deutschen Kulturgeschichte,* Leipzig, 1903.

Bode, Wilhelm, *Kurze Geschichte der Trinksitten und Mässigkeitsbestrebungen in Deutchland,* Munich, 1896.

Cavan, Sherri, *Liquor License: An Ethnology of Bar Behavior,* Chicago, 1966.

Engels, Friedrich, *Die Lage der arbeitenden Klassen in England.*

———, *Preussischer Schnaps im deutschen Reichstag* (in *Marx-Engels Werke,* vol. 19).

Frauenstädt, Paul, "Altdeutscher Durst im Spiegel des Auslandes" (in *Archiv für Kulturgeschichte,* vol. 7, pp. 257–71).

Frazer, James G., *The Golden Bough.*

Gorham, Maurice, and Dunnett, G., *Inside the Pub,* London, 1950.

Grässe, Theodor, *Bierstudien,* Dresden, 1872.

Hackwood, F. W., *Inns, Ales, and Drinking Customs of Old England*, London, 1909.

Handwörterbuch der Staatswissenschaften, vol. I, Jena, 1909; article, "Alkoholfrage."

Handwörterbuch des deutschen Aberglaubens; article, "Trinken," etc.

Harrison, Brian, *Drink and the Victorians*, London, 1971.

Hoffmann, M., *5000 Jahre Bier*, Frankfurt-am-Main, 1956.

Iles, C. M., *Early Stages of English Public House Regulation* (in *The Economic Journal*, vol. 13, pp. 251–62).

Jeggle, Utz, "Alkohol und Industrialisierung" (in Hubert Cancik, ed.: *Rausch, Ekstase, Mystik*, Düsseldorf, 1978, pp. 78–94).

Kautsky, Karl, "Der Alkoholismus und seine Bekämpfung" series of articles in *Die Neue Zeit*, vol. 2, no. 2, 1891.

King, Frank A., *Beer Has a History*, London, 1947.

Krücke, Carl, "Deutsche Mässigkeitsbestrebungen und -vereine im Re-formationszeitalter" *(Archiv für Kulturgeschichte*, vol. 17, pp. 13–30).

Lecky, William E. H., *A History of England in the 18th Century*, London, 1878.

Löffler, Klemens, Vom Zutrinken (in *Archiv für Kulturgeschichte*, vol. 6, no. 3, pp. 281–88).

————, *Die ältesten Bierbücher (Archiv für Kulturgeschichte*, vol. 7).

Mandelbaum, David G., "Alcohol and Culture" (in *Current Anthropology*, vol. 6, no. 3, pp. 281–88).

Mass Observation, *The Pub and the People: A Worktown Study*, London, 1943.

Mauss, Marcel, *The Gift: Forms and Functions of Exchange in Archaic Societies*, New York, 1967; or in *Sociologie et Anthropologie*, Paris, 1968.

Michel, Carl, *Geschichte des Biers von der ältesten Zeit bis zum Jahre 1900*, Augsburg, 1900.

Monckton, H. A., *A History of English Ale and Beer*, London, 1966.

————, *A History of the English Public House*, London, 1969.

Müller, J., "Über Trinkstuben" (in *Zeitschrift für Kulturgeschichte*, 1857, pp. 719–32).

Bibliography

Patrick, C. H., *Alcohol, Culture, and Society*, Durham, 1952.

Potthof, O. D., and Kossenhaschen, Georg, *Kulturgeschichte der deutschen Gaststätte*, Berlin, 1933.

Rauers, Friedrich, *Kulturgeschichte der Gaststätte*, Berlin, 1941 (2 vols.).

Samuelson, J., *The History of Drink*, London, 1878.

Schiedlausky, Günther, *Essen und Trinken*, Munich, 1956.

Schranka, Eduard Maria, *Ein Buch vom Bier*, Frankfurt-an-der-Oder, 1886.

Schultze, Rudolf, *Geschichte des Weins und der Trinkgelage*, Berlin, 1867.

Specht, Franz Anton, *Gastmähler und Trinkgelage bei den Deutschen*, Stuttgart, 1887.

Spiller, Brian, *Victorian Public Houses*, New York, 1973.

Thomas, Dorothy S., *Social Aspects of the Business Cycle*, London, 1925 (in particular the chapter "Alcoholism and the Business Cycle," pp. 127–32).

Webb, Sidney and Beatrice, *The History of Liquor Licensing*, London, 1903 (reprint, 1963).

Tobacco

Apperson, G. L., *The Social History of Smoking*, New York, 1916.

Böse, Georg, *Im blauen Dunst: Eine Kulturgeschichte des Rauchens*, Stuttgart, 1957.

Cohausen, Johann Heinrich, *Satyrische Gedancken von der Pica Nasi, oder der Sehnsucht der Lüstern Nase. Das ist: Von dem heutigen Missbrauchand schädlichen Effect des Schnupf-Tabacks . . . usw.*, Leipzig, 1720.

Conte Corti, Egon Caesar, *Die trockene Trunkenheit: Ursprung, Kampf und Triumph des Rauchens*, Leipzig, 1930 (includes an extensive bibliography).

Curtis, Mattoon M., *The Story of Snuff and Snuff Boxes*, New York, 1935.

Fairholt, *Tobacco*, London, 1859.

Gleichen-Russwurm, Alexander von, "Der Werdegang der Zigarette" (in E. Garbaty, ed., *Die Zigarette*, Berlin, 1914).

Hill, Dr. J., *Cautions Against the Immoderate Use of Snuff*, London, 1761.

Lickint, Fritz, *Tabak und Organismus*, Stuttgart, 1939.

Lüthgen, G. E., *Der Tabak und das Rauchen in der Kunst*, Cologne, 1914 (?).

Motteley, Charles, *Histoire des révolutions de la barbe des Français*, Paris, 1826.

Pohlisch, Kurt, *Tabak: Betrachtungen über Genuss- und Rauschpharmaka*, Stuttgart, 1954.

Tiedemann, Friedrich, *Geschichte des Tabaks und anderer ähnlicher Genussmittel*, Frankfurt-am-Main, 1854.

Work For Chimney Sweepers, Or A Warning for Tobacconists, London, 1601 (reprint, 1936).

OPIUM, HASHISH, ETC.

Baudelaire, Charles, *Les paradis artificiels*.

———, *Le vin et le hachisch*.

Bean, Philip, *The Social Control of Drugs*, New York, 1974.

Bewley, Th. H., "Control of Drugs and Dependence" (in *Medico-Legal Journal*, vol. 37).

De Quincey, Thomas, *Confessions of an English Opium-Eater*.

Doolittle, Justus, *Social Life of the Chinese*, London, 1868.

Gelpke, Rudolf, *Vom Rausch im Orient und Okzident*, Stuttgart, 1966.

Goldsmith, Margaret, *The Trail of Opium*, London, 1939.

Hayter, Alethea, *Opium and the Romantic Imagination*, London, Berkeley, and Los Angeles, 1968.

Jünger, Ernst, *Annäherungen: Drogen und Rausch*, Stuttgart, 1970.

Scheidt, Jürgen von, *Handbuch der Rauschdrogen*, Munich, 1971.

Scott, J. M., *The White Poppy: A History of Opium*, London, 1969.

Teff, Harvey, *Drugs, Society, and the Law*, Westmead, 1975 (Saxon House Studies).

Terry, Charles E., and Pellens, Mildred, *The Opium Problem*, New York, 1928.

Wissler, Albert, *Die Opiumfrage*, Jera, 1931.

ABOUT THE AUTHOR

WOLFGANG SCHIVELBUSCH is a German historian and social scientist, who divides his time between Berlin and New York. *Tastes of Paradise* is the third and final volume in his provocative exploration of the origins of the modern industrialized consciousness begun in his prizewinning *The Railway Journey* and continued in *Disenchanted Night*.